D1195358

QUILTS

THEIR STORY AND
HOW TO MAKE THEM

QUILTS

Their Story and How to Make Them

Marie D. Webster

A NEW EDITION

with notes and
a biography of the author by

Rosalind Webster Perry

PRACTICAL PATCHWORK
Santa Barbara   California
1990

Practical Patchwork
an imprint of Espadaña Press
P.O. Box 30065
Santa Barbara, CA 93130

© 1990 Rosalind Webster Perry
All rights reserved

Printed in the United States of America

Library of Congress Catalog Card Number: 90-91585

ISBN 0-9620811-5-9 cloth
ISBN 0-9620811-6-7 paperback

CONTENTS

PREFACE

This new edition of *Quilts: Their Story and How to Make Them* celebrates an important milestone in quilt history: the 75th anniversary of the publication of America's first quilt book. Its author, Marie D. Webster, was a nationally recognized quilt designer even before she broke new ground by carefully researching the origins and development of the patchwork quilt. Today, her book still has the power to inform and delight us with its intelligence, charming anecdotes and elegant language.

I first saw a copy of *Quilts* on my tenth birthday, when I unwrapped a beautifully boxed First Edition, a gift from my grandmother. At that time, I was only dimly aware that she had actually written the book herself and had also designed and made the flowered quilts which adorned every bed in our house. I must confess that I did not actually read the book until many years later, when I became curious to discover if there was still interest in her work. I was amazed to find that her patterns were still appearing in popular quilt books and magazines, and her name was prominently featured in the most recent volumes on quilt history.

When I learned that *Quilts* had gone out of print, I decided to bring out this new edition, with the complete original text and illustrations. I have written a biography of the author and added notes, index and an updated bibliography. In the interests of clarity, I have assigned numbers to the illustrations — Plate numbers for the color photographs and Figure numbers for the black and white halftones. Twenty-two new color photographs have been added to the fourteen color pictures of Marie Webster's own quilt designs which illustrated the First Edition.

It has been a special pleasure for me to bring out this new edition as a tribute to my very talented and beloved grandmother. But I could not have completed it without the assistance of many wonderful people who gave generously of their time and expertise to help make my vision a reality.

Let me first extend my heartfelt thanks to my mother, who has shared with me her memories of Marie Webster's life. She treasured her mother-in-law's exquisite quilts, original patterns and other memorabilia, always recognizing their importance, even when quilts were not in fashion. In 1979, she established the Webster Collection at the Indianapolis Museum of Art, which will form the core of the first major exhibit of Marie Webster's quilts, opening in 1991.

A special thanks to Cuesta Benberry for sharing so freely the fruits of her many years of research into Marie Webster's role in the twentieth century's first quilt revival. Thanks also to the quiltmakers and quilt historians who enthusiastically offered both encouragement and valuable information: Jan Reynolds, Bets Ramsey, Pat Nickols, Barbara Brackman, Joe Cunningham, Lee Porter, Joyce Gross, Bev Soderland and Barbara Moll.

I am very grateful for the help I received from a great many librarians, museum curators, friends and relatives, especially from Niloo Paydar, Assistant Curator of Textiles and Costumes at the Indianapolis Museum of Art, from Barbara Love and the Marion Public Library, from Sandi Fox and the American Quilt Research Center; also from Barbara Silver, Robert McPherson, Mrs. H. Edward Rietze, Jr., Evelyn Evans, Cathy Mitchell, Jean Coffman, Mary Ann Edmonds, June McKown, Sheila Betterton, the Victoria and Albert Museum, Stonyhurst College, the Wabash Carnegie Public Library, the Metropolitan Museum of Art, the Museum of American Folk Art, the Pocumtuck Valley Memorial Association, the Kauai Museum and the Art Institute of Chicago.

For graciously allowing their quilts to be photographed, I am indebted to Rosamond S. Eliassen, Mr. and Mrs. Herbert B. Feldmann, Mr. and Mrs. Philip Matter, Mrs. John O. Campbell and the Vigo County Historical Society.

Finally, I would like to thank my daughters, Virginia and Angela, and my sister, Kathie, for cheerfully lending a hand, and most of all, my husband, Dick, for his unfailing moral support and his extensive assistance with the editing, design and production of this book.

Rosalind Webster Perry

COLOR PLATES
Following page 148

Marie Webster Quilts from the First Edition

1. Pink Rose Design
2. The Iris Design
3. The Snowflake Quilt Design
4. The Wind-blown Tulip Design
5. Poppy Design
6. Morning Glories
7. The Dogwood Quilt
8. The Sunflower Quilt
9. Golden Butterflies and Pansies
10. Keepsake Quilt
11. The Wild Rose
12. Daisy Quilt
13. Morning Glory Wreath
14. The Bedtime Quilt

Marie Webster Designs — New Illustrations

15. Patchwork Cushions
16. Grapes and Vines
17. French Baskets
18. Sunflower — detail
19. Bunnies Pattern
20. Bunnies
21. Wreath of Roses
22. Poinsettia
23. Nasturtium Wreath
24. Primrose Wreath

ix

Heirloom Quilts — New Illustrations

BLACK AND WHITE ILLUSTRATIONS

Frontispiece: Indiana Wreath

Additional Illustrations

INDIANA WREATH
Made in 1858. Colours: red, green, yellow, and pink

QUILTS

THEIR STORY AND HOW
TO MAKE THEM

BY
MARIE D. WEBSTER

ILLUSTRATED

GARDEN CITY   NEW YORK
DOUBLEDAY, PAGE & COMPANY
1915

Copyright, 1915, by
DOUBLEDAY, PAGE & COMPANY

*All rights reserved, including that of
translation into foreign languages,
including the Scandinavian*

CONTENTS

xvii

ILLUSTRATIONS IN TEXT

QUILTING DESIGNS

INTRODUCTION

ALTHOUGH the quilt is one of the most familiar and necessary articles in our households, its story is yet to be told. In spite of its universal use and intimate connection with our lives, its past is a mystery which—at the most—can be only partially unravelled.

The quilt has a tradition of long centuries of slow but certain progress. Its story is replete with incidents of love and daring, of sordid pilferings and generous sacrifices. It has figured in many a thrilling episode. The same type of handiwork that has sheltered the simple peasant from wintry blasts has adorned the great halls of doughty warriors and noble kings. Humble maids, austere nuns, grand dames, and stately queens; all have shared in the fascination of the quilter's art and have contributed to its advancement. Cottage, convent, and castle; all have been enriched, at one time or another, by the splendours of patchwork and the pleasures of its making.

In its suitability for manufacture within the home, the quilt possesses a peculiar merit. Although exposed for a full century to the competition of machinery, under the depressing influence of which most of the fireside crafts have all but vanished, the making of quilts as a home industry has never languished. Its hold on the affections of womankind has never been stronger than it is to-day. As a homemaker, the quilt is a most capable tool lying ready at the hand of every woman. The selection of design, the care in piecing, the patience in quilting; all make for feminine contentment and domestic happiness.

There are more quilts being made at the present time—in the great cities as well as in the rural communities—than ever before, and their construction as a household occupation—and recreation—is steadily increasing in popularity. This should be a source of much satisfaction to all patriotic Americans who believe that the true source of our nation's strength lies in keeping the family hearth flame bright.

As known to-day, the quilt is the result of combining two kinds of needlework, both of very ancient origin, but widely different in character.

Patchwork—the art of piecing together fabrics
of various kinds and colours or laying patches of
one kind upon another, is a development of the
primitive desire for adornment. Quilting—the
method of fastening together layers of cloths in
such a manner as to secure firmly the loose materials uniformly spread between them, has resulted
from the need of adequate protection against
rigorous climates. The piecing and patching provide the maker with a suitable field for the display
of artistic ability, while the quilting calls for particular skill in handling the needle. The fusing of
these two kinds of needlework into a harmonious
combination is a task that requires great patience
and calls for talent of no mean order.

To our grandmothers quilt making meant social
pleasure as well as necessary toil, and to their
grandmothers it gave solace during long vigils in
pioneer cabins. The work of the old-time quilters
possesses artistic merit to a very high degree. While
much of it was designed strictly for utilitarian purposes—in fact, more for rugged service than display, yet the number of beautiful old quilts which
these industrious ancestors have bequeathed to us
is very large. Every now and then there comes

to light one of these old quilts of the most exquisite loveliness, in which the needlework is almost painful in its exactness. Such treasures are worthy of study and imitation, and are deserving of careful preservation for the inspiration of future generations of quilters.

To raise in popular esteem these most worthy products of home industry, to add to the appreciation of their history and traditions, to give added interest to the hours of labour which their construction involves, to present a few of the old masterpieces to the quilters of to-day; such is the purpose of this book of quilts.

Marion, Indiana

QUILTS
THEIR STORY AND
HOW TO MAKE THEM

CHAPTER I

PATCHWORK IN ANTIQUITY

THE origin of the domestic arts of all nations is shrouded in mystery. Since accurate dates cannot be obtained, traditional accounts must be accepted. The folklore of any country is always exceedingly interesting and generally has a few kernels of fact imbedded somewhere in its flowers of legend, although some of our most familiar household objects are not even mentioned by tradition. Spinning and weaving, however, are very generously treated in the mythology and folklore of all nations. Nearly every race has some legend in which claim is made to the discovery of these twin arts.

In Biblical lore Naa-mah, a sister of Tubal Cain, belonging to the seventh generation after Cain, is said to have invented both spinning and weaving. This tradition is strengthened by the assertions of some historians that the Phrygians

[3]

were the oldest of races, since their birthplace was in Armenia, which in turn is credited with having the Garden of Eden within its boundaries. The Chinese also can advance very substantial claims that primeval man was born with eyes aslant. They at least have a fixed date for the invention of the loom. This was in 2640 B. C. by Lady of Si-Ling, the wife of a famous emperor, Huang-ti.[1]

The Egyptians who, according to their traditions, sprung from the soil, and who despised the Greeks for their late coming into the human arena, were probably quite as ancient as the Phrygians. It is known positively that in the wonderful valley of the Nile there has lived for more than six thousand years a race remarkable for its inventive faculties and the developing of the industrial arts. In the first dawn of human progress, while his nomadic neighbours roamed carefree about him, the Egyptian toiled steadily, and left the records of his achievements beside his god, the Nile.

When investigating any subject, the ability to see the actual thing itself is more helpful than pages of description. In Egypt are preserved for us thousands of wonderful tombs which serve as storehouses of facts concerning the early civilization of this land. The mummy wrappings reveal very distinctly the development of the textiles and decorative arts. The Egyptians, since the earliest historical times, were always celebrated for their manufacture of linen, cotton, and woollen cloths, and the products of their looms were eagerly sought by surrounding nations. The fine linen and embroidered work, yarns and woollen fabrics of both upper and lower Egypt, were held in the highest esteem.

Sir J. Gerdin Wilkinson, in his history of "Ancient Egypt," tells of their knowledge of dyeing and of the nature of the fabrics found in the tombs: "The quantity of linen manufactured and used in Egypt was very great; and, independent of that made up into articles of dress, the numerous wrappers required for enveloping the mummies, both of men and animals, show how large a supply must have been kept ready for the constant demand at home as well as for that of the foreign market."

"The actual experiments made, with the aid of powerful microscopes . . . on the nature of the fibres of linen and cotton threads, have shown that the former invariably present a cylindrical form, transparent, and articulated, or joined like a cane,

while the latter offer the appearance of a flat rib-
and, with a hem or border at each edge; so that
there is no possibility of mistaking the fibres of
either, except, perhaps, when the cotton is in an
unripe state, and the flattened shape of the centre
is less apparent. The results having been found
similar in every instance, and the structure of the
fibres thus unquestionably determined, the threads
of mummy cloths were submitted to the same test,
and no exception was found to their being linen,
nor were they even a mixture of linen and cotton."

"Another very remarkable discovery of the
Egyptians was the use of mordants. They were
acquainted with the effect of acids on colour, and
submitted the cloth they dyed to one of the same
processes adopted in our modern manufactories;
and while, from his account, we perceive how little
Pliny understood the process he was describing,
he at the same time gives us the strongest evidence
of its truth."

"In Egypt," he says, "they stain cloths in a
wonderful manner. They take them in their original state, quite white, and imbue them, not with
a dye, but with certain drugs which have the power
of absorbing and taking colour. When this is

done, there is still no appearance of change in the cloths; but so soon as they are dipped into a bath of the pigment, which has been prepared for the purpose, they are taken out properly coloured. The singular thing is, that though the bath contains only one colour, several hues are imparted to the piece, these changes depending on the natures of the drug employed; nor can the colour be afterward washed off; and surely if the bath had many colours in it, they must have presented a confused appearance on the cloth." [2]

The ability of the Egyptians to have a variety of colours for use in their embroideries and patchworks contributed much to the beauty of these arts.

Embroidery in various forms, applied to all sorts of objects, was commonly practised throughout ancient Egypt, and the Israelites, at the time of the Exodus, carried their knowledge of the textile arts with them to India. Ezekiel in chapter twenty-seven, verse seven, in telling of the glories of Tyre, says: "Of fine linen with broidered work Egypt was thy sail, that it might be to thee for an ensign." In "De Bello Judaics," by Flavius Josephus, another reference is made to ancient needlework:

[7]

"When Herod the Great rebuilt the temple of Jerusalem nineteen years before our era, he was careful not to omit in the decoration of the sanctuary the marvels of textile art which had been the chief embellishment of the tabernacle during the long wanderings in the desert. Before the doors of the most sacred place he hung a Babylonian tapestry fifty cubits high by sixteen wide: azure and flax, scarlet and purple were blended in it with admirable art and rare ingenuity, for these represented the various elements. Scarlet signified fire; linen, the earth; azure, the air; and purple, the sea. These meanings were derived in two instances from similarity of colour: in the other two from their origin, the earth yielding linen and the sea purple. The whole range of the heavens, except the signs, was wrought upon this veil or hanging. The porticos were also enriched with many coloured tapestries ornamented with purple flowers." [3]

There is very meagre information concerning the character and style of tapestry in Egypt during the rule of the Pharaohs. MM. Perrot and Chipiex, in their "Historic de l'Art dans l'Antiquité," publish a painting containing a hanging of purely ornamental design formed of circles, triangles, and palm leaves reversed. Wilkinson describes an Egyptian hanging—an original, not a reproduction—found in an English collection: "In the centre, on a green ground, stands a boy in white, with a goose beside him; and around this centre a border of red and blue lines; then white figures on a yellow ground; again blue lines and red ornaments; and lastly red, white, and blue embroideries." This is a very ancient example of true applied work combined with embroidery. In the Psalms it is said that Pharaoh's daughter shall be brought to the king in a raiment of needlework and that "her clothing is of wrought gold." [4]

The huge columns, bas-reliefs, and the various architectural details of the early Egyptian buildings were all decorated in vivid colours. The interiors of their temples were also covered with gayly coloured scenes which have preserved for us a most extensive knowledge of their life and customs. Their mummy cases were painted in the most brilliant hues, and often the wrappings of the mummies themselves bore brightly coloured portraits of the deceased. Since the Egyptians lived in an atmosphere of brilliant colour, with ever-shining sun, the bluest of skies, and the purple glow of the desert always before them, it is not surprising that they used their brushes with lavish hand. Every plane surface called for ornamentation, whether on temple or shroud. Their pigments, both mineral and vegetable, were remarkable for their permanence.

The crude and childish way in which the Egyptians applied their paint in distinct patches would lead one to believe that patchwork was included in their earliest needlework, even if no actual proof existed. But all nations have at some period used the needle to copy the masterpieces of great artists. The English, as a typical example of this spirit of imitation, sought on a background of cloth of gold to embroider the saints from the canvas of Fra Angelico. Also the French, in the manufacture of their tapestries, copied the works of many of the old masters. Positive proof of the existence of patchwork, or as some choose to call it, "applied work," in Egypt at a very early period is found on a robe belonging to an early sovereign. This article of apparel was of linen and, in general design, resembled a modern apron. According to Wilkinson, it was "richly ornamented in front with lions' heads and other devices, probably of coloured

SECTION OF FUNERAL TENT OF
AN EGYPTIAN QUEEN
Made in a patchwork of coloured goatskins

FIGURE 1

MODERN EGYPTIAN PATCHWORK
Four cushion covers

FIGURE 2

leather; and the border was formed of a row of asps, the emblem of royalty. Sometimes the royal name with an asp on each side was embroidered upon it." [5]

The most ancient example of patchwork is a coloured gazelle hide presented in the Museum of Cairo. The colours of the different pieces of skin are bright pink, deep golden yellow, pale primrose, bluish green, and pale blue. This patchwork served as the canopy or pall of an Egyptian queen about the year 960 B. C. She was the mother-in-law of Shishak, who besieged and captured Jerusalem shortly after the death of Solomon. On its upper border this interesting specimen has repeated scarabs, cartouches with inscriptions, discs, and serpents. The lower border has a central device of radiating lotus flowers; this is flanked by two narrow panels with cartouches; beyond these are two gazelles facing toward the lotus device. Next to the gazelles on each side is a curious detail consisting of two oddly shaped ducks, back to back; then come the two outer compartments of the border, each of which encloses a winged beetle, or scarabæus, bearing a disc or emblem of the sun. The other main division of the field is spotted in regular order with open blossom forms. There is decided order in the repetition and arrangement of these details, which gives a rather stiff and formal look to the whole design.[6]

To-day Egyptians are making patchwork that is undoubtedly a development of the very art practised in the days of Ptolemy, Rameses, and Cleopatra. They do not use their patchwork to adorn quilts, since these are unknown in the warm Nile valley, but as covers for cushions, panels for screens, and decorations suitable for wall hangings. Generally but two kinds of material are employed in its construction: a rather loosely woven cotton cloth, and a firm, coarse linen. The cottons used are all gayly dyed in plain colours, and the linens are in the natural shades, with perhaps a slight mixture of white. The patchwork designs are typically Egyptian, many pieces being covered with replicas of paintings found on tombs and temples. These paintings are copied as faithfully in colour as in design, even the hieroglyphics being exactly reproduced, and altogether make very striking and effective decorations.

The modern Egyptians have the innate taste and ability of all Orientals for harmonizing colour. Their universal use of black to outline and define

MODERN EGYPTIAN PATCHWORK
Panels for screens

FIGURE 3

MODERN EGYPTIAN PATCHWORK
Panels for wall decoration

FIGURE 4

most of the designs produces a beautiful harmony between otherwise clashing hues. With nearly as many shades at their disposal in cloth as a painter has in paint, they are quite ambitious in their attempts to produce realistic scenes. On some of the best specimens of modern Egyptian patchwork gods and goddesses are shown sitting enthroned surrounded by attendants and slaves bearing trophies of war and chase as offerings to the divine beings. On others, groups of men and women are shown, humbly presenting salvers of fruit and the sacred flower—the lotus—to their gods. Some of the most effective work is decorated with a simple life-size figure of Osiris or Rameses the Great in brilliant colours. A few of the more subdued patchwork designs consist of a solitary scarab, the sacred beetle of the Pharaohs, or an asp or two gracefully entwined. The smaller pieces make practical and admirable cushion covers. There are many attractive shops in Cairo that sell quantities of this gay patchwork, and few tourists leave Egypt without a specimen or two as mementoes of the paintings that give us a glimpse of Egypt's ancient splendour.

While among the ancient Greeks and Romans all the arts of the needle were held in the greatest esteem, comparatively little attention was paid to the adornment of their sleeping apartments. Accounts of early Greek houses state that, while the bedchambers were hung all about with curtains and draperies, these were usually of plain fabrics with little attempt at decoration. Of patchwork or appliqué, as known to the Egyptians and Hebrews, the Greeks and Romans have left us no trace. However, as substantiating the regard shown for needlework by the Greeks and Romans, the following two pleasing myths have come down to us: one, the "Story of Arachne," as related by Ovid; the other from the "Odyssey" of Homer.

Arachne, a most industrious needleworker, had the audacity to contest against Pallas, the goddess of the art of weaving. With her bobbins, Arachne wove such wonderful pictures of the Loves of the Gods that Pallas, conscious of having been surpassed by a mortal, in an outburst of anger struck her. Arachne, humiliated by the blow, and unable to avenge it, hanged herself in despair. Whereupon the goddess relented, and with the intention of gratifying Arachne's passionate love of weaving, transformed her into a spider and bade her weave on forever.[7]

The other interesting incident of ancient times is that of Penelope's patient weaving. It is related that, after one short year of wedded happiness, her husband Ulysses was called to take part in the Trojan War. Not a single message having been received from him by Penelope during his long absence, a doubt finally arose as to his being still alive. Numerous suitors then sought her hand, but Penelope begged for time and sought to put them off with many excuses. One of her devices for delay was that of being very busy preparing a funeral robe for Ulysses' father. She announced that she would be unable to choose another husband until after this robe was finished. Day after day she industriously wove, spending patient hours at her loom, but each night secretly ravelled out the product of her day's labour. By this stratagem Penelope restrained the crowd of ardent suitors up to the very day of Ulysses' return.[8]

CHAPTER II

Patchwork and Quilting During the Middle Ages

IN THE early days of Christianity the various organizations of the mother church took a deep interest in all the textile arts, and we are indebted to the ecclesiastical orders for what progress was made in needlework during the beginning of the Middle Ages. The makers of church hangings and vestments were stimulated by thoughts of the spiritual blessings with which they were assured their work would be rewarded. Much of this early ecclesiastic needlework is extremely elaborate and was always eagerly desired by the holy orders. At one time the craze for gorgeous vestments reached such an extreme that we have record of one worthy bishop chiding his priests because they "carried their religion on their backs instead of in their hearts." [1]

The artistic needlework of the Christian era

consists almost entirely of embroidery; no positive reference to patchwork or quilting being found in western Europe prior to the time of the Crusades. But with this great movement, thousands of the most intelligent men in Europe, urged by religious enthusiasm combined with love of adventure, forced their way into eastern countries whose culture and refinements of living far surpassed their own. The luxuries which they found in Syria were eagerly seized and carried home to all the western lands. Returning Crusaders exhibited fine stuffs of every description that roused the envy of all who obtained a glimpse of them. A vigorous commerce with the east was immediately stimulated. From Syria merchants brought into Italy, Spain, and France silks and cottons to supplement the native linen and wool, and also many kinds of embroidered work of a quality much finer than ever known before. As a result dyeing, weaving, and needlework entered on an era of great development.

Previous to the eleventh century so memorable in the history of the Crusaders, references to quilting and patchwork are few and uncertain, but from that time on these twin arts became more and more conspicuous in the needlecraft of nearly every country in western Europe. This is explained by the stimulus which was given to these arts by the specimens of appliqué hangings and garments brought from Syria, where the natives wrought for centuries the identical applied work carried into Palestine from Egypt in Biblical times by the Hebrews and the Phœnecians.

About the earliest applied work of which we have record were the armorial bearings of the Crusaders. A little later came rather elaborate designs applied to their cloaks and banners. Among other specimens of Old English needlework is a piece of applied work at Stonyhurst College depicting a knight on horseback. That this knight represents a Crusader is beyond question since the cross, the insignia of the cause, is a prominent figure in the ornamentation of the knight's helmet and shield, and is also prominent on the blanket on the horse.[2]

Noticeable progress in the arts of both quilting and appliqué was made during the Middle Ages in Spain. Spanish women have always been noted for their cleverness with the needle, and quite a few of the stitches now in use are credited to them. At the time of King Ferdinand and Queen Isabella, applied work had long been known. Whether

OLD ENGLISH APPLIQUÉ
Figure of a knight on horseback   Thirteenth century

FIGURE 5

FIFTH CENTURY APPLIQUÉ

FIGURE 6

it developed from imitating garments brought home by the returning Crusaders, or was adopted from the Moors, who gave the best of their arts to Spain during the thirteenth and fourteenth centuries, cannot be positively stated. However, it is worthy of notice that whenever the Christian came in contact with the Moor, a great advance in the textile arts of the former could generally be observed. This holds true even down to this day, our eagerness to possess the rugs of Turkey and Afghanistan, and the imitation of these designs in the manufacture of domestic carpets, being a case in point.

During the reign of King Philip II, 1527–1598, the grandees of the Spanish court wore beautifully wrought garments, rich with applied work and embroidery. A sixteenth-century hanging of silk and velvet appliqué, now preserved in Madrid, is typical of the best Spanish work. It is described as having a gray-green silk foundation, on which are applied small white silk designs outlined with yellow cord; alternating with the green silk are bands of dark red velvet with ornamented designs cut from the green silk, and upon which are small pieces of white silk representing berries. Also,

[19]

another handsome specimen of Spanish applied work of the seventeenth century is a linen curtain richly embellished with heraldic emblems couched with gold thread. Horse trappings and reposters, loaded with appliqué flowers cut from gold and silver cloth, were much in evidence among the Spanish nobility of this period.

Of particular interest, as showing how oriental quilting designs filtered into Europe through the intercourse of the early Portuguese traders and missionaries with the East Indies, is the brief mention by Margaret S. Burton of a very elaborate old quilt now in a New York collection: "My next find was a tremendous bed quilt which is used as a portière for double folding doors. It formed part of a collection of hangings owned by the late Stanford White. He claimed there were only four of its kind in existence, and this the only one in America. It is valued at $1,000. It is a Portuguese bed quilt and was embroidered centuries ago by the Portuguese missionary monks sent to India. They were commissioned by their queen to embroider them for her to present as wedding gifts to her favourite ladies-in-waiting." On account of intricacy and originality of design this quilt represents years of patient work. It is hand embroidered in golden coloured floss upon a loosely woven linen which had been previously quilted very closely. The work is in chain stitch, and there are at least fifty different stitch patterns. In the centre panel is the sacred cat of India. Doves bearing olive branches, pomegranates, daisies, and passion flowers are intermingled in the beautiful design.[3]

While the uses of patchwork were known over Europe long before the Renaissance, some credit its introduction, into Italy at least, to the Florentine painter, Botticelli (1446–1510). The applied work, or "thought work," of the Armenians so appealed to him that he used it on hangings for church decoration. Under his influence the use of the applied work, *opus conservetum*, for chapel curtains and draperies was greatly extended.[4] In time these simple patchwork hangings were supplanted by the mural paintings and tapestries now so famous. There are still in existence some rare pieces of Italian needlework of the sixteenth century having designs of fine lace interspersed among the embroidered appliqué of silk.

A homely cousin of the gorgeous *opus con-*

servetum, which has filled its useful though humble office down to the present day, is the heavy quilted and padded leather curtain used in many Italian churches in lieu of a door. Many of the church doors are too massive and cumbersome to be opened readily by the entering worshippers, so they are left constantly open. Leather hangings often several inches thick and quilted with rows of horizontal stitches rather widely spaced, are hung before the open doorways. Even these curtains are often quite stiff and unyielding, so that holding back corners for the passage of both worshipper and tourist forms a favourite occupation for numerous beggars.

Appliqué, described as *opus consutum,* or cut work, was made in Florence and Venice, chiefly for ecclesiastical purposes, during the height of their glory in the fifteenth century.[5] One such piece of Florentine cut work is remarkable for its great beauty and the skill shown in bringing together both weaving and embroidery. "Much of the architectural accessories is loom wrought, while the extremities of the evangelists are all done by the needle; but the head, neck, and long beard are worked by themselves upon very fine linen, and

[22]

afterward put together in such a way that the full white beard overlaps the tunics. . . . For the sake of expedition, all the figures were sometimes at once shaped out of woven silk, satin, velvet, linen, or woollen cloth, and sewed upon the grounding of the article. . . . Sometimes the cut work done in this way is framed, as it were, with an edging either in plain or gilt leather, hempen or silken cord, like the leadings of a stained-glass window." Gold and silver starlike flowers, sewn on appliqué embroideries, were common to Venice and also southern Germany in the fifteenth century.[6]

Belonging to the Italian Renaissance period are some marvellous panels, once part of a curtain, which are now preserved in the South Kensington Museum in London. The foundation of these panels is of beautiful blue damask having applied designs cut from yellow satin. These hangings are described as being very rich in effect and unusually handsome, and nothing in the annals of needlework of their period was more glorious.[7]

A very ingenious patchwork, originating in Italy during the sixteenth century and peculiar to that country and Spain, consisted of patterns

[23]

designed so as to be counter hanging. For example, if one section of a length of such patchwork consisted of a blue satin pattern on a yellow velvet ground, the adjoining section would, through the interchange of materials, consist of a yellow velvet pattern on a blue satin ground. The joints of the patching were overlaid with cord or gimp, stitched down so as to conceal them entirely and give definition to the forms constituting the pattern.[8]

Italian needleworkers were very fond of this "transposed appliqué upon two fabrics," especially when composed of designs of foliage conventionally treated, or of arabesques and scrolls. On a piece of old Milanese damask, figured with violet on violet, appear designs in appliqué cut from two shades of yellow satin. These are remarkable for their powerful relief, suggesting sculpture rather than embroidery, and have been pronounced worthy of the best masters of their time—namely, that period so rich in suggestions of ornament—the seventeenth century.

Closely related to patchwork, but not as commonly used, is "inlay." In the making of this style of decoration one material is not laid on to another, but into it. It is the fitting together of small sections of any desired fabric in a prearranged design. For convenience, all the pieces are placed upon a foundation of sufficient firmness, but which does not appear when the work is finished. Ornamental stitches conceal the seams where the edges meet, and it is especially adapted for making heraldic devices. During the Renaissance it was much used by both Spaniards and Italians, who learned the art from the Moors.[9]

An example of quilting, attributed to the Island of Sicily about the year 1400, is described as being a ground of buff-coloured linen. The raised effect is obtained by an interpadding of wool, and the designs are outlined in brown thread. This entire coverlet is embroidered with scenes from the life of Tristan, who frequently engaged in battle against King Langair, the oppressor of his country. This bit of quilting hangs in the Victoria and Albert Museum in London.[10] Another hanging of the fourteenth century, belonging to the same collection, shows a spirited naval battle between galleys. A striking peculiarity of this hanging is that floral designs are scattered in great profusion among the boats of the combatants.

A patchwork made by the application of bits of

leather to velvet was extensively used in some European countries during the Middle Ages. As leather did not fray and needed no sewing over at the edge, but only sewing down, stitching well within the edge gave the effect of a double outline. This combination of leather and velvet was introduced from Morocco. A wonderful tent of this leather patchwork, belonging to the French king, François I, was taken by the Spanish at the battle of Pavia (1525), and is still preserved in the armoury at Madrid.

Some of the very finest specimens of the quilting of the Middle Ages have been preserved for us in Persia. Here the art, borrowed at a very early period from the Arabs, was developed in an unusual and typically oriental manner. Prayer rugs, carpets, and draperies of linen, silk, and satin were among the products of the Persian quilters.

We are indebted to Mr. Alan S. Cole for the following description of a seventeenth-century Persian quilted bath carpet, now preserved at the South Kensington Museum in London.[11] "This typical Persian embroidery is a linen prayer or bath carpet, the bordering or outer design of which partly takes the shape of the favourite Persian

PERSIAN QUILTED LINEN BATH CARPET
Seventeenth century

FIGURE 7

ARMENIAN PATCHWORK
Illustrating the story of St. George and the dragon, and
other Christian subjects

FIGURE 8

architectural niche filled in with such delicate
scrolling stem ornament as is so lavishly used in
that monument of sixteenth-century Mohammedan
art, the Taj Mahal at Agra.   In the centre of the
carpet beneath the niche form is a thickly blos-
soming shrub, laid out on a strictly geometric or
formal plan, but nevertheless depicted with a fairly
close approach to the actual appearance of bunches
of blossoms and of leaves in nature.   But the
regular and corresponding curves of the stems, and
the ordered recurrence of the blossom bunches,
give greater importance to ornamental character
than to any intention of giving a picture of a tree.
Similar stems, blossoms, and leaves are still more
formally and ornamentally adapted in the border
of the carpet, and to fill in the space between the
border and the niche shape.   The embroidery is of
chain stitch with white, yellow, green, and red
silks.   But before this embroidery was taken in
hand the whole of the linen was minutely stitched."

Worthy of mention is a patchwork panel made
in Resht, Persia, in the eighteenth century: "The
foundation ground is of ivory coloured cloth, and
applied to it, almost entirely covering the ivory
background, are designs cut from crimson, cinna-

mon, pink, black, turquoise, and sapphire coloured cloths, all richly embroidered in marigold and green silk."

The following is a quilt anecdote, typically oriental, which contains a bit of true philosophy. It seems that the hero, Nass-ed-Din Hodja, was a Turkish person who became chief jester to the terrible Tamerlane during his invasion of Asia Minor. He was also the hero, real or imaginary, of many other stories which originated during the close of the fourteenth and the beginning of the fifteenth centuries. His tomb is still shown at Akshekir. The story is given entire as it appeared in "Turkey of the Ottoman" by L. M. Garnett:[12]

HOW THE HODJA LOST HIS QUILT

"One winter's night, when the Hodja and his wife were snugly asleep, two men began to quarrel and fight under the window. Both drew knives and the dispute threatened to become serious. Hearing the noise, the Hodja's wife got up, looked out of the window and, seeing the state of affairs, woke her husband, saying: 'Great heavens, get up and separate them or they will kill each other.' But the Hodja only answered sleepily: 'Wife, dear, come to bed again; on my faith there are no men in the world; I wish to be quiet; it is a winter's night. I am an old man, and perhaps if I went out they might beat me.' The Hodja's wife was a wise woman. She kissed his hands and his feet. The Hodja was cross and scolded her, but he threw the quilt about him, went downstairs and out to where the disputants were, and said to them: 'For the sake of my white beard cease, my sons, your strife.' The men, in reply, pulled the quilt from the Hodja's shoulders and made off with it. 'Very well,' observed the old man. He reëntered, locked the door, and went upstairs. Said his wife: 'You did very well to go out to those men. Have they left off quarrelling?' 'They have,' replied the Hodja. 'What were they quarrelling about, Hodja?' 'Fool,' replied the Hodja, 'they were quarrelling for my quilt. Henceforward my motto shall be, "Beware of serpents."'"

Appliqué, or applied work, has never been used in France to the same extent as in England, even though the French name "appliqué" is more frequently used than any other. However, there is one striking example of appliqué work, of Rhenish or French origin, now hanging in the Victoria and Albert Museum in London. This realistic patchwork represents a fight between an armoured knight mounted on a high-stepping white horse and a ferocious dragon. The designs are arranged in a fashion similar to the blocks in a modern quilt, and depict several scenes showing the progress of the combat. There is also a border covered closely with figures of monks, knights, and ladies.[13]

An extract from "First Steps in Collecting," by Grace M. Vallois, gives an interesting glimpse of an old French attic. An object of great interest to us is the old, unfinished quilt she discovered there: "A rummaging expedition in a French *grenier* yields more treasures than one taken in an English lumber room. The French are more conservative; they dislike change and never throw away anything. Among valuable antiques found in the *grenier* of a Louis XV house in the Pyrenees were some rare curtains of white linen ornamented with designs cut from beautiful old chintz; the edges of the applied designs were covered with tightly twisted cotton cord. Also, in the same room, in a drawer of an old chestnut-wood bureau, was found an unfinished bed quilt very curiously worked. It was of linen with a filling of rather

soft cotton cord about an eighth of an inch wide.
These cords were held in place by rows of minute
stitching of white silk, making the bedcover almost
solid needlework. Besides the quilting there were
at rather wide intervals conventional flowers in
peacock shades of blue and green silk executed in
chain stitch. When found, the needle was still
sticking in one of the flowers, and many were
traced ready for work. The traced lines appear to
have been made with India ink and were very
clear and delicate. What caused the abrupt inter-
ruption of the old quilt no one can tell. It is possible that the great terror of 1793 caused the patient
maker to flee from her unfinished task." [14]

In the countries of northern Europe there is
scarcely any record concerning the art of quilting
and patchwork, and little can be said beyond the
fact that both existed in some form or other. In
Germany the quilt so familiar to us is practically
unknown. In the past appliqué was very little
used, except as cut work, or *opus consutum*, in
blazonments and heraldic devices. The thick
feather beds of medieval Germany were covered
with various kinds of thick comforts filled with
either wool or feathers, and sometimes sparsely

quilted. The only decoration of the comfort consisted of a band of ornamental work, ten to twenty inches wide, usually worked in cross-stitch design with brightly coloured yarns. These bands were generally loose upon the comfort, one edge being held down by the pillow, but occasionally they were sewed to the edge of the bedcover.

In a work on arts and crafts relating to their presence in Sweden, it is written that "woven hangings were used to decorate the timbered walls of the halls of the vikings. They were hung over the temples, and they decorated the timber sepulchres of the dead. When the timbered grave of the Danish queen, Fyra Danabode, who died about 950, was opened, remains of woven woollen cloth were found." As far back as Swedish records go it can be shown that Swedish women wove and sewed figured material.[15]

On account of the cold there is urgent need of wall hangings, and they are used extensively throughout Scandinavia. On festive occasions the stiff, cold appearance of Swedish peasants' homes is transformed by the gay wall coverings to one of hospitality and warmth. The hangings used are made of linen, either painted or embroidered in bright colours. The painted ones are especially interesting as they depict many historical scenes. Allegorical and religious subjects are also used to decorate many of these linen hangings. The Swedes are very patriotic, and on their wall hangings show all the saints clad in typical Swedish costumes. The apostles wear Swedish jack boots, loose collars, and pea jackets; and Joseph, as governor of Egypt, is shown wearing a three-cornered hat and smoking a pipe.

There is a valuable collection of Swedish needlework in the Northern Museum of Stockholm, dating from 1639 to the nineteenth century. Among this collection there are a few small pieces of applied work: some cushions, glove gauntlets, and a woman's handbag. It is possible that patchwork was used more extensively than the museum's display would indicate, but since large pieces are very rarely found, patchwork was evidently not held in the same esteem as embroidery and painting.[16]

CHAPTER III

Patchwork and Quilting in Old England

IN SEARCHING for the beginning of needlework in England, the first authentic date revealed relating directly to this subject is 709, when the Bishop of Sherborne writes of the skill Englishwomen had attained at that time in the use of the needle. Preserved in various museums are some examples of Anglo-Saxon embroidery of uncertain date, that are known to have been made before the Bishop of Sherborne's time. Mention should also be made of the wonderful Bayeux Tapestry. This ancient piece is 227 feet long and twenty inches wide, and is of great historical interest, in that it illustrates events of English history from the accession of Edward the Confessor to the English defeat at Hastings by the Normans in 1066. There is some doubt as to whether this tapestry, which has the characteristic of typical appliqué—namely, the absence of shading—is actually of English workmanship, but it is unquestionably of Anglo-Saxon origin. It was first hung in Bayeux Cathedral in 1476.[1]

It is a generally accepted fact that appliqué and embroidery are closely related and of about equal age, although relatively few examples of the former are preserved in collections of needlework. One of the oldest authentic bits of appliqué is at Stonyhurst College. It represents a knight clad in full armour, mounted on a spirited galloping horse. The horse is covered with an elaborately wrought blanket and has an imposing ornament on his head. The knight wears a headdress of design similar to that of the horse and, with arm uplifted and sword drawn, appears about to attack a foe. This work is well done, and the pose of both man and horse shows spirit. It is said to have been made during the thirteenth century.[2] Preserved to us from this same period is the tattered fragment of a coat worn by Edward, the Black Prince, and which now hangs over his tomb in Canterbury Cathedral. With it are the helmet and gauntlets he wore and the shield he carried. The coat is of a red and blue velvet, now sadly faded, applied to a calico background and closely quilted. It is too elaborate to have been made to

[35]

wear under his armour, and was probably worn during state functions where armour was not required, although it was then customary to wear thickly padded and quilted coats and hoods in order to ease the weight of the heavy and unyielding coats of mail.[3]

Much of the best needlework in England at this early period was for the church. Neither labour nor expense was spared to make the magnificent decorations used in the old cathedrals. Aside from the linens, silks, and velvets used in this construction, much gold and silver bullion was wrought into the elaborate altar hangings, altar fronts, and ecclesiastical vestments. In their ornamentation applied work was freely used, especially on the large hangings draped over the altar.

It was during the earliest period that the Latin name *opus consutum* was commonly used to designate patchwork. Chain stitch also was much used on early English embroidery; to such an extent that it is now of great service as an identification mark to fix the dates of medieval needlework. Chain stitch was dignified by the Latin name *opus anglicanum.*[4] Only the most elaborate and richest of embroideries have been preserved; the reason

being that much of the work was done with silver
and gold threads which were in reality fine wires
of these precious metals.   Being exceedingly costly,
they were given unusual care, many being kept
with the royal plate and jewels.   One specimen
made in 905 by Aelfled, the queen of Edward,
the Elder, is now treasured in Durham Cathedral.
It is described as being "of almost solid gold thread,
so exquisitely embroidered that it resembles a fine
illuminated manuscript," and is indescribably beautiful.[5]   In many instances the fabrics of these old
embroideries have partly fallen away, leaving
only frail fragments of the original material held
together by the lasting threads of gold and
silver.

The great amount of precious metals used in
making the richest garments and hangings sometimes made them objects to be desired by avari-
cious invaders.   In an inventory of the contents
of Cardinal Wolsey's great palace at Hampton
Court there are mentioned, among many other
rare specimens of needlework of that period, "230
bed hangings of English embroidery."   None of
them is now in existence, and it is supposed that
they were torn apart in order to fill the coffers of

some vandal who preferred the metal in them to their beauty as hangings.[6]

Among the sumptuous furnishings belonging to the Tudor period, applied work held a prominent place. Vast spaces of cold palace walls were covered by great wall hangings, archways were screened, and every bed was enclosed with curtains made of stoutly woven material, usually more or less ornamented. This was before the advent of French tapestry, which later supplanted the English appliqué wall draperies. The Tudor period was also the time when great rivalry in dress existed. "The esquire endeavoured to outshine the the knight, the knight the baron, the baron the earl, the earl the king himself, in the richness of his apparel." [7]

In direct contrast to the long inventories of beautiful and valuable clothing, bedcovers, and hangings of the rich, are the meagre details relating to the life and household effects of the landless English peasant. In all probability he copied as far as he was able some of the utilities and comforts used by his superiors. If he possessed a cover for his bed, it was doubtless made of the cheapest woven material obtainable. No doubt the pieced or patched quilt contributed materially to his comfort. In "Arts and Crafts in the Middle Ages," Julia de Wolf Addison describes a child's bed quilt included in an inventory of furniture at the Priory in Durham in 1446, "which was embroidered in the four corners with the Evangelistic symbols." In the "Squier of Lowe Degree," a fifteenth-century romance, there is allusion to a bed of which the head sheet is described as embroidered "with diamonds and rubies bright." [8]

It was during the gorgeous reign of Henry VIII that the finest specimens of combined embroidery and patchwork, now preserved in various museums, were made. It was really patch upon patch, for before the motives were applied to the foundation they were elaborately embroidered in intricate designs; and after being applied, they had their edges couched with gold and silver cord and ornate embroidery stitches. Mrs. Lowes relates in "Old Lace and Needlework" that, during the time of Henry VIII, embroidery, as distinct from garment making, appeared; and every article of wearing apparel became an object worthy of decoration. "Much fine stitching was put into the fine white undergarments of that time, and the overdresses of both men and women became stiff with gold thread and jewels. Much use was made of slashing and quilting, the point of junction being dotted with pearls and precious stones. Noble ladies wore dresses heavily and richly embroidered with gold, and the train was so weighty that train bearers were pressed into service. In the old paintings the horses belonging to kings and nobles wear trappings of heavily embroidered gold. Even the hounds, which are frequently represented with their masters, have collars massively decorated with gold bullion." [9]

Mary, Queen of Scots, was devoted to the needle and was expert in its use. It is said that while in France she learned lace making and embroidery. Many wall hangings, bed draperies, bedcovers, and house linens are the work of her skilful fingers, or were made under her personal direction. A number of examples of her work are now owned by the Duke of Devonshire. It is said also that many of the French costumes and laces of her wardrobe were appropriated by Queen Elizabeth, who had little sympathy for the unfortunate queen. As a solace during long days of loneliness, Queen Mary found consolation in her needle, as

have many women of lower degree before and since
her unhappy time. She stands forth as the most
expert and indefatigable of royal needleworkers.[10]

Hardwick Hall is intimately associated with
Queen Mary's life, and is rich in relics of her industry. In one room named for her there are bed
curtains and a quilt said to be her own work. Extracts from old letters relating to her conduct during captivity show how devoted she was to her
needlework. An attendant, on being asked how
the queen passed her time, wrote, "that all day
she wrought with her nydil and that the diversity
of the colours made the work seem less tedious and
that she contynued so long at it that veray payn
made hir to give over." This shows that fatigue
alone made her desist from her beloved work.[11]

There is a very interesting fragment of a bed
hanging at Hardwick Hall said to have been made
by Queen Mary. It is of applied patchwork, with
cream-coloured medallions curiously ornamented
by means of designs singed with a hot iron upon the light-coloured velvet. The singed birds,
flowers, and butterflies are outlined with black silk
thread. The worked medallions are applied to a
foundation of green velvet, ornamented between

[41]

and around them with yellow silk cord. This is only one of a number of examples of curious and beautiful patchwork still in existence and attributed to the Tudor period.[12]

Queen Elizabeth herself was not devoted to needlework, but judging from the accounts of the gorgeous costumes which she delighted to wear, she was one of its greatest patronesses. It is said that at her death she left one of the most extensive wardrobes of history: in it were more than a thousand dresses, which were most voluminous in style and elaborately trimmed with bullion, pearls, and jewels. Before the precious stones were applied, her garments were solidly covered with gold and silver quilting and embroidery, which made them so heavy as to be a noticeable burden even for this proud and ambitious queen. In Berkeley Castle, as prized mementoes of Queen Elizabeth, are five white linen cushions beautifully embroidered with silver threads and cherry-coloured silk. Also with them is the quilt, a wonderful piece of needlework, that matches the hangings of the bed wherein she slept.[13]

The magnificence of Queen Elizabeth's reign gave great impetus to all kinds of needlework.

France at that time led in the development of fine arts, and furnished many of the skilled workmen employed by the nobility solely as embroiderers. There seemed to be no limit to the ambitions of these workers, and the gorgeous results of their labours were beyond anything attempted after them.

To those who wish to study the work of the Tudor period, Hardwick Hall is recommended as the place where the best specimens have been preserved. To Elizabeth, daughter of John Hardwick, born in 1520, and so poor that her marriage portion as the bride of the Earl of Shrewsbury was only thirty pounds, credit is given for the richness of this collection. She was a woman of great ability in the management of her estates, became very wealthy, and gave employment to many people. Included among her dependents were many needleworkers who plied their trade under rigorous administration. Elizabeth of Shrewsbury was a hard mistress, but not above doing an occasional bit of needlework herself, for some pieces bearing her initials and done with remarkable skill are preserved in the collection. She, as much as any Englishwoman, fostered and developed applied

[43]

patchwork along the ambitious line of pictorial needlework.

In Hardwick Hall are several hangings of pictorial needlework that are very interesting. One of black velvet has a picture of a lady strongly resembling Queen Elizabeth. She carries a book in her hand and at her feet reclines a turbaned Turk. In the background is an ecclesiastical hanging which is embroidered to represent a cathedral window. The realistic effect of the whole picture is gained by the use of coloured silks cut in correct proportions and applied to the velvet foundation; very little embroidery entering into the main composition. Another hanging, also of black velvet, has an even more ambitious design. It is described by M. Jourdain in "The History of English Secular Embroidery" as follows: "The ornamentation on the black velvet is with appliqué in coloured silks consisting of figures under arches. In the centre is 'Lucrecia,' on the left 'Chastite,' and on the right 'Liberalitas.' The oval panel on the right contains a shield bearing the arms of Hardwick." At each end of the hanging are fluted Ionic columns, and a decorated frieze is carried across the top. The figures have grace and beauty;

[44]

OLD ENGLISH HANGING WITH APPLIQUÉ
FIGURES

FIGURE 9

A FINE EXAMPLE OF OLD GERMAN APPLIQUÉ

Now in the Metropolitan Museum, New York

FIGURE 10

the drapery of their robes falls in natural folds; and altogether it is a remarkable picture to have been made with patches.[14]

That this fine collection of medieval needlework is preserved for the admiration of people to-day is due to the faithful execution of the Countess of Shrewsbury's will, in which she left all her household furnishings, entailed as heirlooms, to always remain in her House of Hardwick.

In the interesting Hardwick collection are pieces of beautiful needlework known to have been used by Mary, Queen of Scots, during the years she spent as a prisoner at Tutbury. Her rooms there, furnished in regal splendour, are still kept just as she arranged them. The Earl of Shrewsbury was her custodian, and his wife, the countess, often sat and sewed with the unfortunate queen, both making pastime of their needlework.

During the Middle Ages appliqué was in universal use, and not confined merely to wall hangings, quilts, and bed draperies. It was used to ornament all kinds of wearing apparel, including caps, gloves, and shoes. Special designs were made for upholstery, but because of the hard wear imposed upon stools and chairs but

few specimens of this work have been preserved.

Quilting also came into vogue in the making of
bedspreads, of which great numbers were required
during the winter nights in the poorly heated bedrooms. The quilts intended for service were made
of substantial, well-wearing material. None of
these strictly utilitarian quilts is left, but they
were certainly plentiful. The old chroniclers give
us a glimpse of what the women of these days
cherished by telling us that in 1540 Katherine
Howard, afterward wife of Henry VIII, was presented with twenty-three quilts of Sarsenet, closely
quilted, from the Royal Wardrobe.[15]

Tradition says that, during the reign of Henry
VIII, the much used and popular "black work" or
"Spanish work" was introduced into England by
his Spanish wife, Catherine of Aragon. It has been
found that this work did not originate in Spain but
was taken there probably by the Moors or by the
Crusaders, for it is known to have been perfected at
a very remote period in both Persia and China. The
following interesting description of black work is
from Mrs. Lowes' "Chats on Old Lace and Needlework":

"The work itself was a marvel of neatness, precision, and elegant design, but the result cannot be said to have been commensurate with the labour of its production. More frequently the design was of scrollwork, worked with a fine black silk back stitching or chain stitch. Round and round the stitches go, following each other closely. Bunches of grapes are frequently worked solidly, and even the popular peascod is worked in outline stitch, and often the petit point period lace stitches are copied, and roses and birds worked separately and afterward stitched to the design." There are many examples of this famous "Spanish work" in the South Kensington Museum in London. Quilts, hangings, coats, caps, jackets, smocks, are all to be seen, some with a couched thread of gold and silver following the lines of the scrolls. This is said to be the Spanish stitch referred to in the old list of stitches, and very likely may be so, as the style and manner are certainly not English; and we know that Catherine of Aragon brought wonders of Spanish stitchery with her, and she herself was devoted to the use of the needle. The story of how, when called before Cardinal Wolsey and Campeggio, to answer to King Henry's accusations, she had a skein of embroidery silk round her neck, is well known.[16]

"The black silk outline stitchery on linen lasted well through the late seventeenth and eighteenth centuries. Very little of it is seen outside the museums, as, not being strikingly beautiful or attractive, it has been destroyed. Another phase of the same stitchery was working cotton and linen garments, hangings and quilts in a kind of quilted pattern with yellow silk. The finest materials were used, the padding being placed bit by bit into its place. The quilting work was made in tiny panels, illustrating shields and other heraldic devices, and had a surface as fine as carved ivory. When, as in the case of one sample at South Kensington, the quilt is additionally embroidered with fine floss silk flowers, the effect is very lovely." [17]

One interesting feature of "black work" and similar flat embroideries was their constant use in decorating furnishings for the bedroom. It was peculiarly well adapted for quilts, as its rather smooth surface admirably resisted wear.

Fashions in needlework changed, but not with the same rapidity as in clothing. Gradually ideas and customs from other countries crept into England and new influences were felt. An established trade with the Orient brought Eastern products to her markets, and oriental designs in needlework became popular. About this time "crewel" was much in vogue. This was embroidery done with coloured woollen threads and was a step backward in the art. Some of this "crewel" work, done in the seventeenth century, is described by M. Jourdain in "English Secular Embroidery": "These hangings, bed curtains, quilts, and valances are of linen or a mixture of cotton and linen, and one type is embroidered with bold, freely designed patterns in worsted. They are worked almost always in dull blues and greens mixed with more vivid greens and some browns, but rarely any other colouring." [18]

A very curious custom of these days was the use of "mourning beds," with black hangings, coverlets, and even sheets. As these funereal articles of furniture were quite expensive, it was a friendly custom to lend these mourning beds to families in time of affliction. In 1644 Mrs. Eure wrote to Sir Ralph Verney: "Sweet Nephew, I am now overrun with miserys and troubles, but the greatest misfortune that could happen to me was the death of the gallantest man (her husband) that I ever

[49]

knew." Whereupon Sir Ralph, full of sympathy, "offers her the loan of the great black bed and hangings from Claydon." [19]

Interesting indeed are descriptions of wonderful old quilts that are now guarded with zealous care in English museums. One, an original and striking design, is closely quilted all over in small diamonds. Upon it is embroidered an orange tree in full leaf and loaded with fruit. This tree, together with the fancy pot in which it is planted, covers practically the entire quilt. In the lower corners a gentleman is shown picking oranges and a lady in a patient attitude is waiting to receive them, the figures of both being scarcely taller than the flower pot. The whole design is made up of gayly coloured silks evidently worked in after the quilting was done. Mention is also made of an elaborate quilt said to be the work of Queen Anne, which is preserved at Madresfield Court. Sarah, Duchess of Marlborough, in giving an order for house furnishings for her "wild, unmerciful house" about 1720, asks for "a vast number of feather beds, some filled with swansdown, and a vast number of quilts." [20]

Mrs. Delany, who lived from 1700 to 1788, and left a large correspondence relating to needlework, which was later edited by Lady Llanover, was a most prolific worker with her needle as well as a profuse letter writer. She was often quoted as an authority and given credit for much originality in her designs. A quilt that she made is described as follows: "Of white linen worked in flowers, the size of nature, delineated with the finest coloured silks in running stitch, which is made use of in the same way as by a pen etching on paper; the outline was drawn with pencil. Each flower is different, and evidently done at the moment from the original." Another quilt of Mrs. Delany's was made upon a foundation of nankeen. This was unique in that no colours were used besides the dull yellow of the background. Applied designs of leaves tied together with ribbons, all cut from white linen and stitched to the nankeen with white thread, made a quilt no wise resembling the silken ones of earlier periods. This quilt may be termed a forerunner of the vast array of pieced and patched washable quilts belonging to the nineteenth century. [21]

The embroidering of quilts followed the process of quilting, which afforded the firm foundation essential for heavy and elaborate designs. There were many quilts made of white linen quilted with yellow silk thread, and afterward embroidered very tastefully with yellow silk floss. Terry, in the history of his "Voyage to the East Indies," made about the middle of the seventeenth century, says: "The natives show very much ingenuity in their manufactures, also in making excellent quilts of their stained cloth, or of fresh-coloured taffeta lined with their prints, or of their satin with taffeta, betwixt which they put cotton wool, and work them together with silk." [22]

Among many articles in a list of Eastern products, which Charles I, in 1631, permitted to be brought to England, were "quilts of China embroidered in Gold."[23] There is a possibility that these quilts were appreciated quite as much for the precious metal used in the embroidery as for the beauty of design and workmanship. It was but a short time after this that women began to realize how much gold and silver had gone into all forms of needlework. They looked upon rare and beautiful embroidery with greedy eyes, and a deplorable fashion sprang up, known in France as "parfilage" and in England as "drizzling." This was nothing more or less than ripping up, stitch by stitch, the magnificent old hangings, quilts, and even church vestments, to secure gold and silver thread. Lady Mary Coke, writing from the Austrian Court, says: "All the ladies who do not play cards pick gold. It is the most general fashion I ever saw, and they all carry their bags containing the necessary tools in their pockets. They even begged sword knots, epaulettes, and galons that they might add more of the precious threads to the spool on which they wound the ravelled bullion, which they sold." To the appreciative collector this seems wanton sacrilege. [24]

John Locke, 1632–1704, a very famous man of Charles II's time, and one of the greatest philosophers and ardent champions of civil and religious rights which England ever produced, mentioned quilts in his "Thoughts Concerning Education." In telling of the correct sort of beds for children he writes as follows: "Let his Bed be hard, and rather Quilts than Feathers. Hard Lodging strengthens the Parts, whereas being buryed every Night in Feathers melts and dissolves the Body. . . . Besides, he that is used to hard Lodging at Home will not miss his Sleep (where he has most Need of it) in his travels

[53]

Abroad for want of his soft Bed, and his Pillows laid in Order." [25]

Pepys, a contemporary of Locke, in his incomparable and delicious Diary, remarks: "Home to my poor wife, who works all day like a horse, at the making of her hanging for our chamber and bed," thus telling us that he was following the fashion of the day in having wall, window, and bed draperies alike. It is plain, too, by his frequent "and so to bed," that his place of sleep and rest was one of comfort in his house. [26]

A quilt depending solely upon the stitching used in quilting, whether it be of the simple running stitch, the back stitch, or the chain stitch, is not particularly ornamental. However, when viewed at close range, the effect is a shadowy design in low relief that has a distinctive but modest beauty when well done. Early in the eighteenth century a liking for this fashion prevailed, and was put to a variety of uses. Frequently there was no interlining between the right and wrong sides. At Canons Ashby there are now preserved some handsome quilted curtains of this type, belonging to Sir Alfred Dryden, Baronet. [27]

During the Middle Ages instruction in the use

of the needle was considered a necessary part of the English girl's education. By the seventeenth century "working fine works with the needle" was considered of equal importance with singing, dancing, and French in the accomplishments of a lady of quality. In the eighteenth century much the same sentiment prevailed, and Lady Montagu is quoted as saying: "It is as scandalous for a woman not to know how to use a needle as for a man not to know how to use a sword." [28]

The *Spectator* of that time sarcastically tells of two sisters highly educated in domestic arts who spend so much time making cushions and "sets of hangings" that they had never learned to read and write! A sober-minded old lady, grieved by frivolous nieces, begs the *Spectator* "to take the laudable mystery of embroidery into your serious consideration," for, says she, "I have two nieces, who so often run gadding abroad that I do not know when to have them. Those hours which, in this age, are thrown away in dress, visits, and the like, were employed in my time in writing out receipts, or working beds, chairs, and hangings for the family. For my part I have plied the needle these fifty years, and by my good-will would never

[55]

have it out of my hand. It grieves my heart to see a couple of proud, idle flirts sipping the tea for a whole afternoon in a room hung round with the industry of their great-grandmothers." [29] Another old lady of the eighteenth century, Miss Hutton, proudly makes the following statement of the results of years of close application to the needle: "I have quilted counterpanes and chest covers in fine white linen, in various patterns of my own invention. I have made patchwork beyond calculation." [30]

Emblems and motifs were great favourites with the quilt workers of "ye olden times" and together with mottoes were worked into many pieces of embroidery. The following mottoes were copied from an old quilt made in the seventeenth century: "Covet not to wax riche through deceit," "He that has lest witte is most poore," "It is better to want riches than witte," "A covetous man cannot be riche." [31]

The needle and its products have always been held in great esteem in England, and many of the old writers refer to needlework with much respect. In 1640 John Taylor, sometimes called the "Water Poet," published a collection of essays, etc., called

"The Needle's Excellency," which was very popular in its day and ran through twelve editions. In it is a long poem entitled, "The Prayse of the Needle." The following are the opening lines: [32]

"To all dispersed sorts of Arts and Trades
  I write the needles prayse (that never fades)
  So long as children shall begot and borne,
  So long as garments shall be made and worne.
  So long as Hemp or Flax or Sheep shall bear
  Their linnen Woollen fleeces yeare by yeare;
  So long as silk-worms, with exhausted spoile,
  Of their own entrailes for man's gaine shall toyle;
  Yea, till the world be quite dissolved and past,
  So long at least, the Needles use shall last."

It is interesting to read what Elizabeth Glaister, an Englishwoman, writes of quilts in England: [33]

"Perhaps no piece of secular needlework gave our ancestors more satisfaction, both in the making and when made, as the quilt or bed coverlet. We have seen a good many specimens of them, both of the real quilted counterpanes, in which several thicknesses of material were stitched together into a solid covering, and the lighter silken or linen coverlets ornamented with all sorts of embroidery. Cradle quilts also were favourite pieces of needlework and figure in inventories of Henry VIII's time.

"The real quilts were very handsome and the amount of labour bestowed on them was enormous. The seventeenth century was a great time for them, and the work of this period is generally very good. The quilting of some of them is made by sewing several strands of thick cotton between the fine linen of the surface and the lining. When one line was completed the cotton was laid down again next to it, and another line formed.

"A sort of shell pattern was a favourite for quilting. When a sufficient space was covered with the ground pattern, flowers or other ornaments were embroidered on this excellent foundation. Perhaps the best results as a work of art were attained when both quilting and flowers were done in bright yellow silk; the effect of this colour on a white ground being always particularly good. A handsome quilt may be worked with a darned background. It is done most easily on huckaback towelling of rather loose weave, running the needle under the raised threads for the ground.

"A very effective quilt in quite a different style is made in applied work on unbleached cotton sheeting. A pattern of yellow fruit or flower with leaves is cut out in coloured serges sewn on with crewels in buttonhole stitch; stems, veins, and buds being also worked in crewels, and the ground slightly darned in dim yellow crewel. It is elaborate, but a very pleasant and repaying piece of work.

"Many beautiful old quilts are made of silk and satin embroidered in pure silks or in gold and silver twist. Most of the best specimens are from France and Italy, where from the arrangement of the houses the beds have continued to be more *en evidence* than has been the case in England for the last two centuries. Many also are of Indian origin; the ground of these is sometimes of fine soft silk and sometimes of thick muslin, over which the pattern is worked in silk. Others, though of Indian workmanship, show a European influence, of which the most curious are those worked at Goa, under Portuguese dominion in the seventeenth century."

CHAPTER IV

THE QUILT IN AMERICA

THE date of the quilt's advent into America is unknown, and—because of the lack of knowledge concerning the house furnishings of the early colonists—can never be positively determined. Quilts were in such general use and were considered as such ordinary articles that the early writers about family life in the colonies neglected to mention them. We do know, however, that quilted garments, bedspreads, curtains, and the like were very essential to the comfort and well-being of the original settlers along the Atlantic seaboard.[1]

Extensive investigation has shown that the introduction of the arts of patchwork and quilting to the American continent is due entirely to the English and the Dutch. No evidence has been found that Spanish or French colonists made use of quilting. The Spaniards in the warm lands of

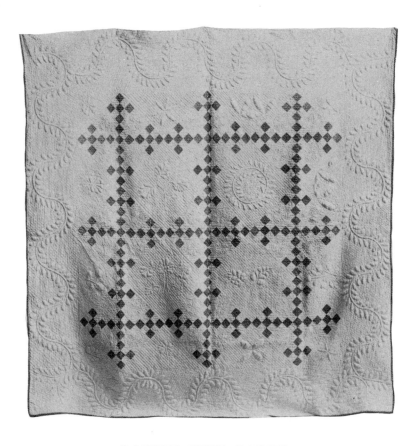

DOUBLE NINE PATCH

Made in Ohio in 1808.   Colours: blue and white, and beautifully quilted

FIGURE 11

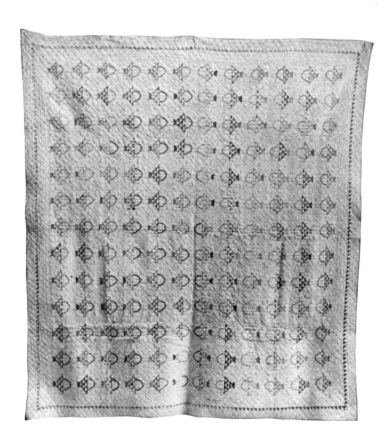

PIECED BASKETS

A design much used by the old-time quilt makers.   This quilt, which is about
85 years old, is unusual, in that the baskets are so small

FIGURE 12

the South had little real need of warm clothing, and
—outside of possible appliqué heraldic devices on
the coats of the early explorers—may be considered as having brought to the New World none
of the art so popular in Spain at the time. The
French who opened up Canada brought none of
the quilting or patchwork of France with them.
While needlework was taught at a very early date
in the convents of Quebec, it was apparently only
the more fanciful kinds of embroidery. As a protection against the biting northern winters, the
early French settlers sought protection under furs,
which could be obtained quite readily in the great
woods. To secure more bed clothing, it was very
much easier to engage in a little hunting than to
go through the laborious processes of piecing and
quilting. To both Spanish and French, the new
world was strictly a man's country—to adventure
in and win riches upon which to retire to a life of
ease in their native lands. With them, therefore,
the inspiration of founding a home and providing
it with the comforts of life was lacking; and without
such inspiration the household arts could never
flourish.

The English and Dutch planted their colonies

along the coast from Virginia to Massachusetts with the primary object of founding new homes for themselves. With them came their wives and daughters, who brought along as their portion such household comforts and conveniences as they possessed. Under their willing hands spinning, weaving, and the manufacture of garments began immediately. Their poorly heated log houses made necessary an adequate supply of bedding and hangings for protection against the winter cold. Substantial, heavy curtains, frequently lined and quilted, were hung over both doors and windows and were kept closely drawn during the bitter winter nights. In the more imposing homes were silk damask curtains with linings of quilted silk to keep out the drafts of cold that swept through the rooms.

In Massachusetts in the early colonial days quilted garments, especially petticoats, were in general use. It is a curious circumstance that we owe this bit of information largely to the description of runaway slaves. The Boston *News Letter* of October, 1707, contains an advertisement describing an Indian woman who ran away, clad in the best garments she could purloin from her mistress's wardrobe: "A tall Lusty Carolina Indian

[62]

Woman, named Keziah Wampun Had on a striped red, blue and white Home-spun Jacket and a Red one, a Black and quilted White Silk Crape Petticoat, a White Shift and also a blue with her, and a mixt Blue and White Linsey Woolsey Apron." In 1728 the *News Letter* published an advertisement of a runaway Indian servant who, wearied by the round of domestic drudgery, adorned herself in borrowed finery and fled: "She wore off a Narrow Stript pinck cherredary Gown turned up with a little floured red and white Callico. A Stript Home-spun quilted petticoat, a plain muslin Apron, a suit of plain Pinners and a red and white flowered knot, also a pair of green stone earrings, with white cotton stockings and leather heel'd wooden shoes."

A few items in a list of articles ordered from England for a New England bride, Miss Judith Sewall, who was married in 1720, give some idea of what was considered as a suitable wedding outfit during that period. The bride belonged to a rich family and no doubt had furnishings much more extensive than usual: "A Duzen of good Black Walnut Chairs, A Duzen Cane Chairs, and a great chair for a chamber, all black Walnut. One Duzen large

Pewter Plates, new fashion, a Duzen Ivory-hafted knives and forks. Four Duzen small glass salt cellars, Curtains and Vallens for a Bed with Counterpane, Head Cloth, and Tester made of good yellow watered camlet with Trimming. Send also of the same camlet and trimming as may be enough to make cushions for the chamber chairs. A good fine larger Chintz quilt, well made." This list also includes such items as kitchen utensils, warming pans, brass fenders, tongs, and shovels, and "four pairs of large Brass candlesticks." [2]

As the resources of the new country were developed, the women were given some respite from their spinning, weaving, and garment making. Much of their hard-won leisure was spent piecing quilts. In the rigorous climate of bleak New England there was great need of warm clothing and bedding, and the spare moments of the housekeeper were largely occupied in increasing her supply. To make the great amount of bedding necessary in the unheated sleeping rooms, every scrap and remnant of woollen material left from the manufacture of garments was saved. To supplement these, the best parts of worn-out garments were carefully cut out, and made into quilt pieces.

INTERIOR OF BEDROOM
Cochran residence, Deerfield, Mass., showing colonial bedstead with quilt and canopy

FIGURE 13

JACOB'S LADDER

One of the most striking of the quilts having Biblical names.   Colours: blue
and white

FIGURE 14

Beautiful, even gorgeous, materials were imported for costumes of the wives and daughters of the wealthy colonists. There may be a greater variety of fabrics woven to-day, but none is more splendid in texture and colour than those worn by the stately ladies of colonial times. The teachings of the strict Puritans advocated plainness and simplicity of dress; even the ministers in the churches preached against the "sinfulness of display of fine raiment." Notwithstanding the teachings and pleadings of the clergy, there was great rivalry in dress among the inhabitants of the larger colonial towns. "Costly thy habit as thy purse can buy," was unnecessary advice to give to the rich colonist or to his wife. Men's attire was also of costly velvets lined with handsome brocades; beautifully embroidered waistcoats, silk stockings, and gold lace trimmings were further additions to their costumes during the pre-Revolutionary period.

After these gay and costly fabrics had served their time as wearing apparel, they were carefully preserved and made over into useful articles for the household. The pinch of hard times during the struggle for independence made it imperative for many well-to-do families to economize. Consequently, in many old patchwork quilts may be found bits of the finest silks, satins, velvets, and brocades, relics of more prosperous days.

Alice Morse Earle, in her charming book on "Home Life in Colonial Days," gives us a rare insight into our great-grandmothers' fondness for patchwork, and how highly they prized their bits of highly coloured fabrics:

"The feminine love of colour, the longing for decoration, as well as pride in skill of needlecraft, found riotous expression in quilt making. Women revelled in intricate and difficult patchwork; they eagerly exchanged patterns with one another; they talked over the designs, and admired pretty bits of calico and pondered what combinations to make, with far more zest than women ever discuss art or examine high art specimens together to-day. There was one satisfactory condition in the work, and that was the quality of cottons and linens of which the patchwork was made. Real India chintzes and palampores are found in these quilts, beautiful and artistic stuffs, and the firm, unyielding, high-priced, 'real' French calicoes.

"Portions of discarded uniforms, old coat and cloak linings, brilliantly dyed worn flannel shirts

and well-worn petticoats were component parts of
quilts that were needed for warmth. 'A magnificent scarlet cloak, worn by a Lord Mayor of London and brought to America by a member of the
Merrit family of Salisbury, Massachusetts, went
through a series of adventures and migrations and
ended its days as small bits of vivid colour, cast-
ing a grateful glory and variety on a patchwork
quilt in the Saco Valley of Maine.

"Around the outstretched quilt a dozen quilters
could sit, running the whole together with fanciful
set designs of stitchery. Sometimes several quilts
were set up, and I know of a ten days' quilting bee
in Narragansett in 1752." [3]

The women who came from Holland to make
their homes on the narrow island at the mouth
of the Hudson were housekeepers of traditional
Dutch excellence. They delighted in well-stocked
linen closets and possessed unusual quantities of
sheets, pillow cases, and bedding, mostly of their
own spinning and weaving. Like their English
neighbours to the north, in Connecticut and Massachusetts, they adopted quilted hangings and garments for protection against the severity of winter.
Their quilted petticoats were the pride and joy of

[67]

these transplanted Hollanders, and in their construction they exerted their highest talents in
design and needlework. These petticoats, which
were worn short enough to display the home-
knitted hose, were thickly interlined as well as
quilted. They were very warm, as the interlining
was usually of wool. The fuller the purse, the
richer and gayer were the petticoats of the New
Amsterdam dames. [4]

While not so strict in religious matters as their
Puritan neighbours, the early inhabitants of New
Amsterdam always observed Sunday and attended
church regularly. Within the fort at the battery
stood the church, built of "Manhattan Stone" in
1642. Its two peaked roofs with the watch-tower
between was the most prominent object of the
fortress. "On Sunday mornings the two main
streets, Broadway and Whitehall, were filled with
dignified and sedate churchgoers arrayed in their
best clothes. The tucked-up panniers worn by
the women displayed to the best advantage the
quilted petticoats. Red, blue, black, and white
were the favourite and predominating colours,
and the different materials included fine woollen
cloth, camlet, grosgrain silk, and satin. Of all the

CONVENTIONAL TULIP

Made in Ohio about 1840. Beautifully quilted in medallions and pine-
apples of original design. Colors: red, pink, and green.

FIGURE 15

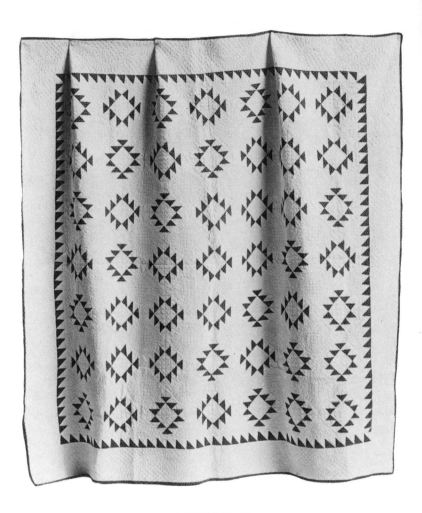

DOUBLE X
A modern quilt. Colours: blue and white

FIGURE 16

articles of feminine attire of that period the quilted petticoat was the most important. They were worn short, displaying the low shoes with high heels and coloured hose with scarlet clockings; silken hoods partially covered their curled and powdered hair; altogether a charming and delightful picture." [5]

The low, flat land of South Manhattan lying along the Hudson, because of its similarity to their mother country, was a favourite dwelling-place in New Netherlands. This region, known as Flatbush, was quickly covered with Dutch homes and big, orderly, flourishing gardens. A descendant of one of the oldest Dutch families which settled in this locality, Mrs. Gertrude Lefferts Vanderbilt, in her book, "The Social History of Flatbush," has given many interesting details of early New York life. She tells of the place quilt making held in the community, and how the many intricate patterns of patchwork pleasantly occupied the spare moments of the women, thus serving as a means of expression of their love of colour and design. The following little domestic picture shows how conveniently near the thrifty housewife kept her quilt blocks: "A low chair with a

[69]

seat of twisted osier, on which was tied a loose feather-filled cushion, covered with some gay material. On the back of these chairs hung the bag of knitting, with the little red stocking and shining needles plainly visible, indicating that this was the favourite seat of the industrious mother of the family; or a basket of patchwork held its place upon a low stool (bankje) beside the chair, also to be snatched up at odd intervals (ledige tyd)." [6]

One reliable source of information of the comforts and luxuries that contributed to pleasant dwelling in old New York is found in old inventories of household effects. Occasionally complete lists are found that throw much light on the furnishings of early days. Such an inventory of the household belongings of Captain John Kidd, before he went to sea and turned pirate, mentions over sixty different kinds of house furnishings, from a skillet to a dozen chairs embellished with Turkish embroidery. Among the articles with which John Kidd and his wife Sarah began housekeeping in New York in 1692, as recorded in this inventory, were four bedsteads, with three suits of hangings, curtains, and valances to go with them. Feather beds, feather pillows, linen sheets, tablecloths, and napkins, ten blankets, and three quilts. How much of this store of household linens was part of his wife's wedding dower is not stated.[7]

The early settlers in Virginia and the Carolinas were mostly English of the better class, who had been landed proprietors with considerable retinues of servants. As soon as these original colonists secured a firm foothold, large estates were developed on which the manners and customs of old England were followed as closely as possible. Each plantation became a self-supporting community, since nearly all the actual necessities were produced or manufactured thereon. The loom worked ceaselessly, turning the wool, cotton, and flax into household commodities, and even the shoes for both slave and master were made from home-tanned leather. For their luxuries, the ships that carried tobacco and rice to the English markets returned laden with books, wines, laces, silverware, and beautiful house furnishings of every description.

In the colonial plantation days of household industry quilts, both patchwork and plain, were made in considerable numbers. Quilts were then in such general use as to be considered too commonplace to be described or even mentioned. Consequently, we are forced to depend for evidence of their existence in those days on bills of sale and inventories of auctions. These records, however, constitute an authority which cannot be questioned.

In 1774 Belvoir, the home of the Fairfax family, one of the largest and most imposing of houses of Virginia, was sold and its contents were put up at auction. A partial list of articles bought at this sale by George Washington, then Colonel Washington, and here given, will show the luxury to which the Southern planter was accustomed: "A mahogany shaving desk, settee bed and furnishings, four mahogany chairs, oval glass with gilt frame, mahogany sideboard, twelve chairs, and three window curtains from dining-room. Several pairs of andirons, tongs, shovels, toasting forks, pickle pots, wine glasses, pewter plates, many blankets, pillows, bolsters, and *nineteen coverlids*." [8]

It was customary in the good old days after a dinner or ball for the guests, who necessarily came from long distances, to stay all night, and many bedrooms, frequently from ten to twenty-five, besides those needed for the family, were provided in the big houses. All were beautifully furnished

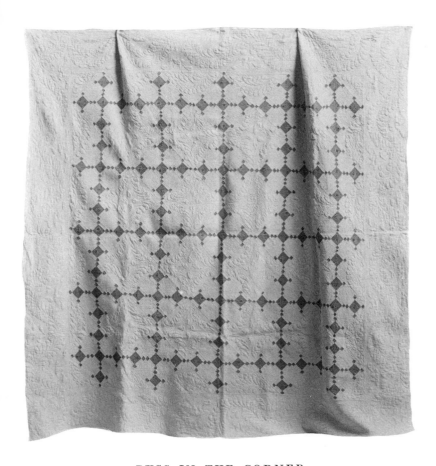

PUSS-IN-THE-CORNER

A beautifully quilted design made about 1855.   Colours: a dull green calico
having small red flowers and white

FIGURE 17

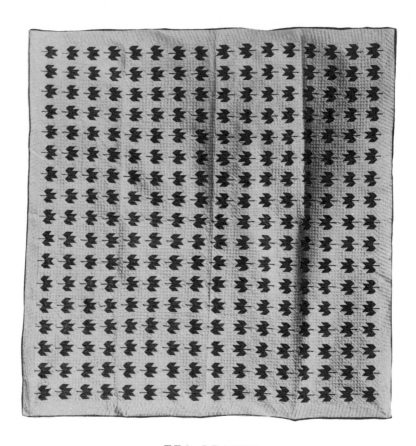

TEA LEAVES

A quaint old design combining a pieced block with an applied leaf stem.
Colours: green and white

FIGURE 18

with imported, massive, carved furniture from France and England. In one year, 1768, in Charlestown, South Carolina, occurred twelve weddings among the wealthy residents of that city, and all the furniture for these rich couples came from England. The twelve massive beds with canopies supported by heavily carved posts, decorated with rice stalks and full heads of grain, were so high that steps were needed in order to climb into them. Elaborate and expensive curtains and spreads were furnished to correspond. In one early inventory of an extensively furnished house there are mentioned "four feather beds, bolsters, two stools, looking-glass tipt with silver, two Turkey carpets, one yellow mohair bed counterpane, and *two green silk quilts.*" From this it is evident that the quilt had already found its place, and no doubt in great numbers, on account of the many beds to furnish in the spacious house of the rich planters.

Shortly after the Revolution came the great migration from Virginia over the ridges of the Blue and the Appalachian chains into what was then the wilderness of Tennessee and Kentucky. The descendants of these hardy pioneers who first forced their way westward still live among the

Kentucky and Virginia hills under the conditions which prevailed a hundred years ago. In this heavily timbered rough country they manage to eke out a precarious existence by cultivating small hillside patches of cotton, corn, and a few vegetables. Immured in the seclusion of the mountains they have remained untouched by the world's progress during the past century. Year after year they are satisfied to live this secluded existence, and but rarely make an acquaintance with a stranger. Educational advantages, except of the most elementary sort, are almost unknown, and the majority of these mountaineers neither read nor write. As a result of this condition of isolated and primitive living, existing in the mountains of Virginia, Kentucky, Tennessee, and the Carolinas, the household crafts that flourished in this country before the advent of machinery are still carried on exactly as in the old days.

The simple needs of the family are almost entirely supplied by the women of the household. They spin, weave, and make the few plain garments which they and their families wear. Day after day, year in and year out, these isolated women must fill in the hours with little tasks connected with

home life. As in many other instances where women are dependent upon their own resources for
amusement, they have recourse to their needles.
Consequently, it is in the making of quilts, coverlets,
and allied forms of needlework that these mountain women spend their hours of recreation.

The quilts, both pieced and patched, that are
made in mountaineers' cabins have a great variety
of designs. Many designs have been used again
and again by each succeeding generation of quilters
without any variation whatever, and have well-
known names. There are also designs that have
been originated by a proficient quilt maker, who has
made use of some common flower as the basis for her
conventional design. It has not been a great many
years since the materials used in making the mountain quilts were dyed as well as woven in the home.
The dyes were homemade from common roots and
shrubs gathered from nearby woods and meadows.
Blue was obtained from wild indigo; brown from
walnut hulls; black from the bark of scrub-oak; and
yellow from laurel leaves. However, the materials which must be purchased for a quilt are so
meagre, and the colours called "oil boiled"—now
used to dye calico—are so fast, that the mountain

women seldom dye their own fabrics any more. They bring in a few chickens or eggs to the nearest village, and in exchange obtain a few yards of precious coloured calico for their quilts. [9]

Miss Bessie Daingerfield, a Kentuckian, who is in close touch with these mountaineers, tells us what a void the quilt fills in the lives of the lonely women of the hills:[10] "While contemporary women out in the world are waging feminist war, those in the mountains of the long Appalachian chain still sit at their quilting frames and create beauty and work wonders with patient needles. There is much beautiful and skilful handiwork hidden away in these hills. The old women still weave coverlets, towels, and table linen from wool from their own sheep and from flax grown in their own gardens. The girls adorn their cotton gowns with 'compass work,' exact, exquisite. In some places the men and boys, girls and women, make baskets of hickory reeds and willows to delight the heart of the collector. But from the cradle to the grave, the women make quilts. The tiny girl shows you with pride the completed four patch or nine patch, square piled on square, which 'mammy aims to set up for her ag'inst spring.' The mother tells you

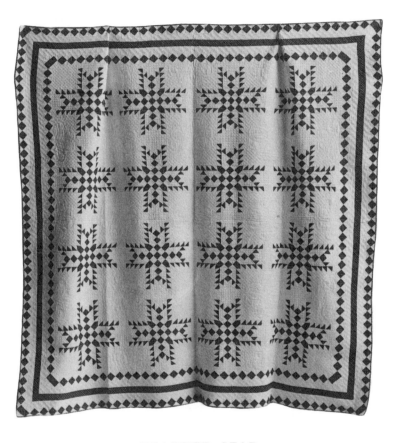

FEATHER STAR
Made about 1850.   Colours: blue and white

FIGURE 19

DRUNKARD'S PATH

A modern quilt after an old pattern. Colours: light blue
and white

FIGURE 20

half jesting, half in earnest, 'the young un will
have several ag'inst she has a home of her own.'
No bride of the old country has more pride in her
dower chest than the mountain bride in her pile of
quilts. The old woman will show you a stack of
quilts from floor to ceiling of her cabin. One dear
old soul told me she had eighty-four, all different,
and 'ever' stitch, piecin', settin' up, quiltin', my
own work and ne'er another finger tetched hit.'"

Patchwork was an important factor in making
plain the knotty problems of existence, as Eliza
Calvert Hall clearly shows when she makes "Aunt
Jane of Kentucky" say: "How much piecin' a
quilt is like livin' a life! Many a time I've set and
listened to Parson Page preachin' about predestination and free will, and I've said to myself, 'If I
could jest git up in the pulpit with one of my quilts
I could make it a heap plainer to folks than parson's makin' it with his big words.' You see, you
start out with jest so much caliker; you don't go
to the store and pick it out and buy it, but the
neighbours will give you a piece here and a piece
there, and you'll have a piece left over every time
you cut a dress, and you take jest what happens to
come. And that's like predestination. But when

it comes to the cuttin' out, why, you're free to choose your own pattern. You can give the same kind o' pieces to two persons, and one'll make a 'nine patch' and one'll make a 'wild-goose chase,' and there'll be two quilts made out of the same kind of pieces, and jest as different as they can be. And that is jest the way with livin'. The Lord sends us the pieces, but we can cut them out and put 'em together pretty much to suit ourselves, and there's a heap more in the cuttin' out and the sewin' than there is in the caliker." [11]

In the great Central West, from Ohio to the Mississippi, the early settlers passed through the same cycle of development as did their ancestors in the beginnings of the original colonies along the seaboard. The same dangers and privations were faced, and the women, as well as the men, quickly adapted themselves to the hardships of life in a new country. Shortly after the War of 1812, which secured to the United States a clear title to this vast region, the great migration into the Ohio Valley began. Some families came by way of the Great Lakes, some by wagon over the Pennsylvania ridges, and still others by horseback over the mountains from Virginia. One and all of these pioneer families brought with them their most cherished household possessions. It is hardly necessary to say that every family had one or more quilts among its household goods. Many cases are on record of rare old mahogany bureaus and bedsteads transported hundreds of miles over trails through the wilderness on pack horses. Upon arrival at the site chosen for the future home, the real work of house building and furnishing began.

"Only he who knows what it means to hew a home out of the forest; of what is involved in the task of replacing mighty trees with corn; only he who has watched the log house rising in the clearing, and has witnessed the devotedness that gathers around the old log schoolhouse and the pathos of a grave in the wilderness, can understand how sobriety, decency, age, devoutness, beauty, and power belong to the story of those who began the mighty task of changing the wild west into the heart of a teeming continent." Thus Jenkin Lloyd Jones, in his address on "The Father of Lincoln," gives a graphic picture of the labours and trials confronting those who made the first settlements in what are now the flourishing states of Ohio, Indiana, Kentucky, Illinois, and Michigan.[12]

[79]

As in the colonies of New England, so here, the comforts of the family depended upon the thrift, energy, and thoughtfulness of the women. Practically every article of clothing worn by the entire family, as well as all household supplies, were the work of their busy hands. All day in the frontier cabin could be heard the hum of the spinning wheel, the clack of the loom, or the click of knitting needles. In many localities the added work of teaching the children fell to the mothers, and the home lessons given around the fireplace, heaped with glowing logs, were the only ones possible for many boys and girls. It is of particular interest to note how often learning and housekeeping went hand in hand in the first homes of this new country. The few lines following are extracts from the diary of a busy Indiana housewife of the period preceding the Mexican War, and show how fully occupied was the time of the pioneer woman:

"November 10th. To-day was cider-making day, and all were up at sunrise."

"December 1st. We killed a beef to-day, the neighbours helping."

"December 4th. I was much engaged in try-

STAR OF THE EAST

Elaborate pineapple quilting designs in the corners.   Colours:
red and white

FIGURE 21

WHITE QUILT WITH TUFTED BORDER
Now in Metropolitan Museum, New York

FIGURE 22

ing out my tallow. To-day I dipped candles and finished the 'Vicar of Wakefield.'"

"December 8th. To-day I commenced to read the 'Life of Washington,' and I borrowed a singing book. Have been trying to make a bonnet. The cotton we raised served a very good purpose for candle-wicking when spun." [13]

In the Middle West, without friendly coöperation, the lot of the pioneer would have been much more difficult than it was. Julia Henderson Levering tells of the prevalence of this kindly custom in her interesting "Historic Indiana": "The social pleasures of the earliest days were largely connected with the helpful neighbourhood assistance in the homely, necessary tasks of the frontier. If a new cabin was to be built, the neighbours assembled for the house raising, for the logs were too heavy to be handled alone. When a clearing was made, the log rolling followed. All men for miles around came to help, and the women to help cook and serve the bountiful meals. Then there were corn huskings, wool shearings, apple parings, sugar boilings, and quilting bees." [14]

About 1820 a new channel of commerce was opened to the inhabitants of the Ohio Valley, in the advantages of which every household shared. This was the establishing of steamboat and flatboat communication with New Orleans. From out of the Wabash River alone over a thousand flatboats, laden with agricultural products, passed into the Ohio during the annual spring rise on their way to the seaport by the Gulf of Mexico. On their return voyage these boats were laden with sacks of coffee, quaint Chinese boxes of tea, china and silk from France, and mahogany and silver from England. In this manner the finest fabrics, which were hitherto obtainable only in those cities that possessed sea communication, were available in every river hamlet. Many of the fine old quilts now being brought to light in the Central West were wrought of foreign cloth which has made this long journey in some farmer's scow.[15]

In England during the middle of the past century, the Victorian period was known chiefly for its hideous array of cardboard mottoes done in brilliant wools, crochet tidies, and wax flowers. It is particularly fortunate that at this time the women of the United States were too fully occupied with their own household arts and industries to take up with the ideas of their English sisters.

By far the best needlework of this period were the beautiful quilts and bedspreads, exquisite in colour and design, which were the product of American women. The finest quilts were wrought along designs largely original with the quilters themselves, who plied their needles in solitary farmhouses and out-of-the-way hamlets to which the influence of English idea in needlework could not penetrate. In no locality in our country can so many rare and beautiful quilts be found as in the Middle West. Many of the best were made during those early days of struggle for mere existence, when they served the busy housewife as the one precious outlet for her artistic aspirations.

The type of quilt that may be called distinctively American was substantial in character; the material that entered into its construction was serviceable, of a good quality of cotton cloth, or handwoven linen, and the careful work put into it was intended to stand the test of time. The coloured materials combined with the white were also enduring, the colours being as nearly permanent as it was possible to procure. Some cottons were dyed by the quilt makers themselves, if desirable fast shades could not be readily procured otherwise. The fundamental idea was to make a quilt that would withstand the greatest possible amount of wear. Some of the artistic possibilities in both colour and design were often subordinated to the desire to make quilts as nearly imperishable as possible. The painstaking needlework required to produce a quilt deserved the best of material for its foundation. Silks, satins, velvets, and fine linen and cotton fabrics of delicate shades were not favoured as quilt material by the old-time needle-workers, who wrought for service first and beauty afterward.

A most beautiful example of the American quilt at its best is found in the "Indiana Wreath." Its pleasing design, harmonious colours, and exquisite workmanship reveal to us the quilter's art in its greatest perfection. This quilt was made by Miss E. J. Hart, a most versatile and skilful needle-woman, in 1858, as shown by the small precise figures below the large wreath. The design is exceedingly well balanced in that the entire quilt surface is uniformly covered and no one feature is emphasized to the detriment of any other. The design element of the wreath is a compact group of flowers, fruit, and leaves, which is repeated ten

SUNBURST AND WHEEL OF FORTUNE
Comparatively modern quilts.   Colours: blue and white

FIGURE 23

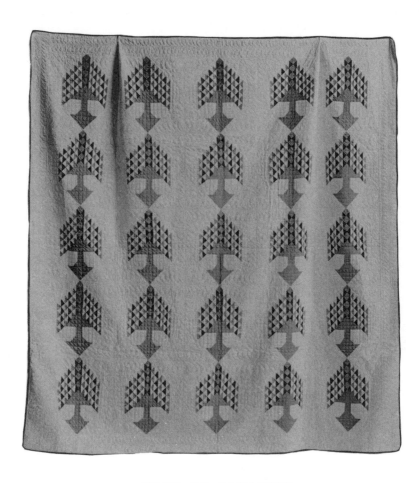

TREE OF PARADISE
Made in Indiana over 75 years ago.   Colours: red and green

FIGURE 24

times in making the complete circle. The vase filled with drooping sprays, flowers, and conventionalized buds forms an ideal centre for this wreath. Curving vines intermingled with flowers make a desirable and graceful border. This quilt is a little more than two and a half yards square, and the central wreath fills a space equal to the width of a double bed, for which it was evidently intended.

Miss Hart displayed unusual ability in choosing and combining the limited materials at the disposal of the quilt maker in a newly settled region. The foundation is fine white muslin; the coloured material is calico, in the serviceable quality manufactured at that time, and of shades considered absolutely fast, then known as "oil boiled." Only four colours are used in the design: green, red, yellow, and pink, the latter having a small allover printed design in a darker shade.

Miss Hart planned her quilting quite carefully. In the large blank spaces in the corners are placed special, original designs that have some features of the much-used "feather" pattern. Aside from these triangular corner designs all the quilting is in small diamonds, which form a very pleasing background for the effective coloured designs. The maker's name and the date are closely quilted in white in plain bold-faced type just below the wreath. In the centre of the wreath, in neat script in black thread, is quilted the name "Indiana Wreath," and all the stitchery of top and quilting is the very perfection of quilt making.[16]

The beautiful white quilts that are treasured as relics of past industry by their fortunate owners deserve special mention. They are rare because nowadays no one will expend the large amount of time necessary to complete one. The foundation of such a quilt is fine white muslin, or fine home-spun and woven linen, with a very thin interlining. The beauty of the quilt depends upon the design drawn for the quilting and the fine stitches with which the quilting is done. There is usually a special design planned for these white quilts which includes a large central panel or pattern, with smaller designs for the corners embodying some of the ideas of the central panel. Around these decorative sections the background is so closely quilted as to resemble a woven fabric. This smooth, even background throws the principal designs into low relief. After the entire quilt is

[86]

OLD BED WITH QUILT AND CANOPY AND TRUNDLE BED BENEATH

Now in Memorial Hall, Deerfield, Mass.

FIGURE 25

TWO WHITE TUFTED BEDSPREADS
Both made in Pennsylvania about 100 years ago

FIGURE 26

quilted and removed from the frames, the main design is frequently further accentuated by having all the most prominent features, such as the leaves and petals of flowers, stuffed. To accomplish this tiny holes are made on the wrong side of each section of the design and cotton is pushed in with a large needle until the section is stuffed full and tight. This tedious process is followed until every leaf and petal stands out in bold relief.

The fashion which has prevailed for many years of dressing beds all in white has no doubt caused the destruction of many beautiful quilts. The white quilts that have been preserved are now considered too valuable to be subjected to hard wear. The most exquisite ones were made in the last of the eighteenth and the beginning of the nineteenth centuries.

It was the rage for white bed coverings that shortened the lives of many old pieced and patched quilts of good colouring. The "Country Contributor" tells of her experiences in dressing up the white beds: [17]

"I remember with regret the quilts I wore out, using them white side up in lieu of white Marseilles spreads. The latter we were far too poor to own:

[87]

the 'tufted' ones had worn out; and I loathed the cheap 'honeycombed' cotton things we were forced to use unless we were going to be frankly 'poor' and cover our beds with plain patchwork, made up hurriedly and quilted in simple 'fans' in plebeian squares, as poor folk who haven't time for elegant stitches did theirs. So I used the old quilts, making their fine stitches in intricate patterns serve for the design in a 'white spread,' turning the white muslin lining up. A beautiful white spread it made, too, I realize now, more fully than I did then, though I now would know much better than to turn the wonderful appliqué stars and flowers and wheels from view. Strange, is it not, that we relinquish so much of life's best joy and pleasure before we know what actually is good?" This fashion prevails to-day, in some instances insisted upon for sanitary reasons, but it has lost to us many of the finest examples of quilting that existed because where there were no coloured patterns to relieve the white expanse, the quilting had to be perfect. If you have a white quilt treasure it, for competent quilters are no longer numerous and few there are who can reproduce it.

TUFTED BEDSPREAD WITH KNOTTED FRINGE

A design of very remarkable beauty.   Over 100 years old

FIGURE 27

UNKNOWN STAR

A New England quilt about 115 years old. Colours: once bright red
and green are now old rose and dull green. The original
quilting designs are very beautiful

FIGURE 28

CHAPTER V

How Quilts Are Made

IT IS only in comparatively recent years that many articles of wearing apparel and house furnishings have been manufactured outside the home. One after another, spinning, weaving, shoemaking, candlemaking, tailoring, knitting, and similar tasks have been taken from the home-keeper because the same articles can be made better and cheaper elsewhere. The housewife still keeps busy, but is occupied with tasks more to her liking. Among the few home occupations that have survived is quilting. With many serviceable substitutes it is not really necessary for women to make quilts now, but the strange fascination about the work holds their interest. Quilt making has developed and progressed during the very period when textile arts in the home have declined under the influence of the factory. More quilts are being made at the present time and over a wider area than ever before.

Quilts, as known and used to-day, may be divided into two general classes, washable and non-washable, depending upon the materials of which they are made. The methods for constructing each class are the same, and are so very simple that it seems hardly necessary to explain them.

The name quilt implies two or more fabrics held together with many stitches. Webster defines a quilt as "Anything that is quilted, especially as a quilted bedcover or a skirt worn by women; any cover or garment made by putting wool, cotton, etc., between two cloths and stitching them together." The verb, to quilt, he defines as "To stitch or to sew together at frequent intervals in order to confine in place the several layers of cloth and wadding of which a garment, comforter, etc., may be made. To stitch or sew in lines or patterns."

The "Encyclopædia Britannica" is a little more explicit and also gives the derivation of the name, quilt, as follows: "Probably a coverlet for a bed consisting of a mass of feathers, down, wool, or other soft substances, surrounded by an outer covering of linen, cloth, or other material." In its earlier days the "quilt" was often made thick and sewed as a form of mattress. The term was

also given to a stitched, wadded lining for body armour. "The word came into English from old
French *cuilte*. This is derived from Latin *culcitra*,
a stuffed mattress or cushion. From the form *culcitra* came old French *cotra*, or *coutre* whence *coutre
pointe;* this was corrupted into counterpoint, which
in turn was changed to counterpane. The word
'pane' is also from the Latin *pannus*, a piece of
cloth. Thus 'counterpane,' a coverlet for a bed,
and 'quilt' are by origin the same word."

Broadly speaking, from these definitions, any
article made up with an interlining may be called
a quilt. However, usage has restricted the meaning
of the word until now it is applied to a single form
of bed covering. In the United States the distinction has been carried even farther and a quilt
is understood to be a light weight, closely stitched
bedcover. When made thicker, and consequently
warmer, it is called a "comfort."

The three necessary parts of a quilt are the top,
the lining or back, and the interlining. The top,
which is the important feature, unless the quilting
is to be the only ornamentation, may be a single
piece of plain cloth; or it may be pieced together
from many small pieces different in size, colour,

and shape, so as to form either simple or fanciful designs. The top may also be adorned with designs cut from fabrics of varying colours and applied to the foundation with fancy stitches, or it may be embroidered. The materials may be either cotton, linen, wool, or silk. The back is usually of plain material, which requires no description. The interlining, if the quilting is to be close and elaborate, must be thin. If warmth is desired a thicker interlining is used and the lines of quilting are spaced farther apart. The design of the top and the quilting lend themselves very readily to all manner of variations, and as a result there is an almost infinite variety of quilts.

For convenience in making, nearly every quilt is composed of a number of blocks of regular form and size which, when joined together, make the body of the quilt. Each of these blocks may have a design complete in itself, or may be only part of a large and complicated design covering the whole top of the quilt.

There is a radical distinction between the verbs "to piece" and "to patch," as used in connection with the making of quilts. In this instance the former means to join together separate pieces of

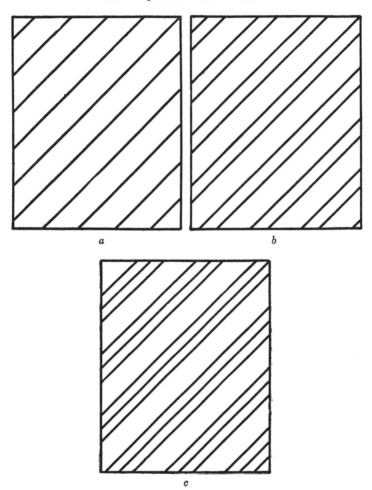

a   *b*

c

QUILTING DESIGNS
(*a*) Single Diagonal Lines   (*b*) Double Diagonal Lines
(*c*) Triple Diagonal Lines

like material to make sections or blocks that are in turn set together to form the top of the quilt. The pieces are usually of uniform shape and size and of contrasting colours. They are sewed together with a running stitch, making a seam upon the wrong side. The quilt called "Star of the East" is an excellent example of a pieced quilt in which a number of small pieced sections are united to form a single design that embraces the entire top of the quilt.

Patches are commonly associated with misfortune. The one who needs them is unfortunate, and the one who has to sew them on is usually an object of sympathy, according to a wise old saw: "A hole may be thought to be an accident of the day, but a patch is a sure sign of poverty." But patch quilts belong to a different class than the patches of necessity, and are the aristocrats of the quilt family, while the pieced quilts came under the heading of poor relations.

However, this term is a misnomer when applied to some pieced quilts. Many of the "scrap quilts," as they are called in some localities, are very pretty when made from gay pieces—carefully blended—of the various shades of a single colour. The stars in the design called "The Unknown Star" are made of a great variety of different patterns of pink calico, yet the blending is so good that the effect is greatly heightened by the multiplicity of shades.

Pieced quilts make a special appeal to women who delight in the precise and accurate work necessary in their construction. For those who enjoy making pieced quilts, there is practically no limit to the variety of designs available, some of which are as intricate as the choicest mosaic. The bold and rather heavy design known as "Jacob's Ladder" is a good example of the pieced quilt. Another is the "Feathered Star," whose lightness and delicacy make it a most charming pattern. The pieced quilt with one large star in the centre, called by some "The Star of the East" and by others "The Star of Bethlehem," is a striking example of mathematical exactness in quilt piecing. In quilts made after this pattern all the pieces must be exactly the same size and all the seams must be the same width in order to produce a perfect star.

The French word "appliqué" is frequently used to describe the patched or laid-on work. There is no single word in the English language that exactly translates "appliqué." The term "applied work" comes nearest and is the common English term. By common usage patchwork is now understood to mean quilt making, and while used indiscriminately for both pieced and patched quilts, it really belongs to that type where the design is cut from one fabric and applied upon another. "Sewed on" and "laid quilts" are old terms given to appliqué or patched quilts.

The distinction between "pieced" and "patched" quilts is fittingly described by Miss Bessie Daingerfield, the Kentuckian who has written interestingly of her experiences with mountain quilt makers. She says: "To every mountain woman her piece quilts are her daily interest, but her patch quilts are her glory. Even in these days, you women of the low country know a piece quilt when you see one, and doubtless you learned to sew on a 'four-patch' square. But have you among your treasures a patch quilt? The piece quilt, of course, is made of scraps, and its beauty or ugliness depends upon the material and colours that come to hand, the intricacy of the design, and one's skill in executing it. I think much character building must be done while hand and eye coöperate to make, for example, a star quilt with its endless tiny points

COMBINATION ROSE
More than 85 years old.   Colours: rose, pink, and green

FIGURE 29

DOUBLE TULIP

Made in Ohio, date unknown. The tulips are made of red calico covered
with small yellow flowers. The roses have yellow centres

FIGURE 30

for fitting and joining, but a patch quilt is a more
ambitious affair. For this the pattern is cut from
the whole piece and appliquéd on unbleached cotton. The colours used are commonly oil red, oil
green, and a certain rather violent yellow, and
sometimes indigo blue. These and these only are
considered reliable enough for a patch quilt, which
is made for the generations that come after. The
making of such a quilt is a work of oriental patience." [1]

"Appliqué work is thought by some to be an
inferior kind of embroidery, although it is not. It
is not a lower but another kind of needlework in
which more is made of the stuff than of the stitching. In appliqué the craft to the needleworker is
not carried to its limit, but, on the other hand, it
calls for great skill in design. Effective it must be:
coarse it may be: vulgar it should not be: trivial
it can hardly be: mere prettiness is beyond its
scope: but it lends itself to dignity of design and
nobility of treatment." The foregoing quotation
is from "Art in Needlework" by Louis F. Day
and Mary Buckle. It is of interest because it
explains how appliqué or "laid-on" needlework ranks
with other kinds. [2]

After all the different parts of a quilt top are either pieced or decorated with applied designs, they are joined together with narrow seams upon the wrong side of the quilt. If a border is included in the design it should harmonize in colour and design with the body of the quilt. However, in many quilts, borders seem to be "a thing apart" from the remainder of the top and, apparently, have been added as an afterthought to enlarge the top after the blocks had been joined. In old quilts a border frequently consisted of simple bands of colours similar to those found in the body of the quilt, but more often new material entirely different in colour and quality was added when greater size was desired. Many old quilts were three yards or more square, generous proportions being very essential in the old days of broad four-posters heaped with feather beds.

The top being completed, the back or lining, of the same dimensions as the top, is next made of some light-weight material, usually white cotton. The quilt, to quote the usual expression, is then "ready for the frames." In earlier days the quilting frame could be found in every home, its simple construction making this possible. In its usual

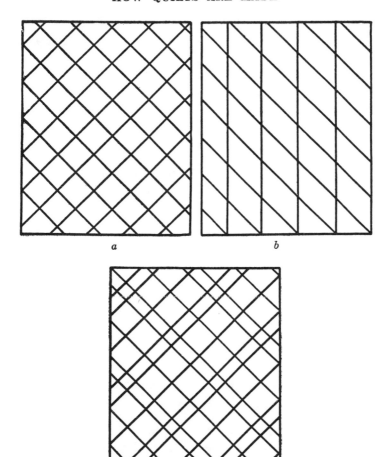

a

b

c

QUILTING DESIGNS

(a) Diamonds   (b) Hanging Diamonds   (c) Broken Plaid

[99]

form it consists of four narrow pieces of wood, two somewhat longer than a quilt, and two shorter, perhaps half as long, with holes bored in the ends of each piece. These pieces are made into an oblong frame by fastenings of bolts or pegs, and are commonly supported on the backs of chairs. More pretentious frames are made with round pieces for the sides, and with ends made to stand upon the floor, about the height of a table, these ends having round holes into which the side pieces fit. Such a frame is then self-supporting and frequently has a cogwheel attachment to keep the sides in place and to facilitate the rolling and unrolling of the quilt. The majority of frames are very plain, but occasionally a diligent quilter is encountered who has one made to suit her particular requirements, or has received an unusually well-built one as a gift. One old frame worthy of mention was made of cherry with elaborate scroll designed ends, cherry side bars, and a set of cogwheels also made of cherry; all finished and polished like a choice piece of furniture.

Each side bar or roll of the quilting frame is tightly wound with cotton strips or has a piece of muslin firmly fastened to its entire length, to

PRINCESS FEATHERS

Made in Indiana about 1835.   Colours: soft dull green and old rose

FIGURE 31

PRINCESS FEATHERS WITH BORDER

Notice the maple leaf inserted in the border. Colours: red and green

FIGURE 32

which is sewed the edges of the lining, one side to each bar. Then the extra length is rolled up on one side of the frame, and after being tightly stretched, the wooden pieces are securely fastened. On this stretched lining or back of the quilt, the cotton or wool used for filling or interlining is spread very carefully and smoothly; then with even greater care the top is put in place, its edge pinned or basted to the edge of the lining, and drawn tightly over the cotton. The ends of the quilt must also be stretched. This is done by pinning pieces of muslin to the quilt and wrapping them around the ends of the frame. Great care is required to keep all edges true and to stretch all parts of the quilt uniformly.

Upon this smooth top the quilting is drawn, for even the most expert quilters require outlines to quilt by. If the quilt top is light in colour the design is drawn with faint pencil lines; if the colours are too dark to show pencil markings, then with a chalked line. It is a fascinating thing to children to watch the marking of a quilt with the chalk lines. The firm cord used for this is drawn repeatedly across a piece of chalk or through powdered starch until well coated, then held near the quilt, and very tightly stretched, while a second person draws it up and lets it fly back with a snap, thus making a straight white line. How closely the lines are drawn depends wholly upon the ambition and diligence of the quilter. The lines may be barely a quarter of an inch apart, or may be placed only close enough together to perform their function of keeping the interlining in place.

Patterns of quiltings are not as plentiful as designs for the patchwork tops of quilts; only about eight or ten standard patterns being in general use. The simplest pattern consists of "single diagonal" lines, spaced to suit the work in hand. The lines are run diagonally across the quilt instead of parallel with the weave, in order that they may show to better advantage, and also because the cloth is less apt to tear or pull apart than if the quilting lines are run in the same direction as the threads of the fabric. The elaboration of the "single" diagonal into sets of two or more parallel lines, thus forming the "double" and "triple" diagonals, is the first step toward ornamentation in quilting. A further advance is made when the quilting lines are crossed, by means of which patterns like the "square," "diamond," and "hanging diamond" are produced.

Wavy lines and various arrangements of hoops, circles, and segments of circles are among the more complex quilting patterns, which are not particularly difficult. Plates and saucers of various diameters are always available to serve as markers in laying out such designs. The "pineapple," "broken plaid," and "shell" patterns are very popular, especially with those who are more experienced in the art. One very effective design used by many quilters is known as the "Ostrich Feather." These so-called feathers are arranged in straight bands, waved lines, or circles, and— when the work is well done—are very beautiful. The "fan" and "twisted rope" patterns are familiar to the older quilters but are not much used at the present time.

Frequently the quilting design follows the pieced or patched pattern and is then very effective, especially when a floral pattern is used. Some quilters show much originality and ingenuity in incorporating into their work the outlines of the flowers and leaves of the quilt design. Sometimes the pieced top is of such common material as to seem an unworthy basis for the beautiful work of an experienced quilter, who stitches with such

QUILTING DESIGNS

(a) Rope   (b) Shell   (c) Fan

QUILTING DESIGNS
(a) Feathers in Bands   (b) Feathers in Waved Lines
(c) Feathers in Circles

[105]

patient hand, wasting, some may think, her art upon too poor a subject. However, for the consolation of those who consider quilting a wicked waste of time, it may be added that nowadays expert quilters are very few indeed, and enthusiasts who have spent weeks piecing a beautiful quilt have been known to wait a year before being able to get it quilted by an expert in this art.

On the thin cotton quilts that have the elaborate quilting designs and are the pride of the owner, the quilting is done with fine cotton thread, about number seventy. The running stitch used in quilting should be as small and even as it is possible for the quilter to make. This is a very difficult feat to accomplish, since the quilt composed of two thicknesses of cloth with an interlining of cotton is stretched so tightly in the frame that it is quite difficult to push the needle through. Also the quilter, while bending over the frame with one hand above and one hand below, is in a somewhat unnatural strained position. It requires much patience to acquire the knack of sitting in the rather uncomfortable quilter's position without quickly tiring.

Skill and speed in quilting can be acquired only

PEONIES

About 75 years old.   Made for exhibition at state fairs in the Middle West.
Colours: red, green, and yellow

FIGURE 33

NORTH CAROLINA LILY

Over 80 years old.   Flowers: red and green; the border has green buds with
red centres.   The quilting designs are remarkable for
their beauty and originality

FIGURE 34

through much practice. Perfect quilting cannot be turned out by a novice in the art, no matter how skilful she may be at other kinds of needle-work. The patience and skill of the quilter are especially taxed when, in following the vagaries of some design, she is forced to quilt lines that extend away from her instead of toward her. As the result of many years spent over the quilting frame, some quilters acquire an unusual dexterity in handling the needle, and occasionally one is encountered who can quilt as well with one hand as with the other.

Quilting is usually paid for by the amount of thread used, no consideration being given to the amount of time expended on the work. A spool of cotton thread, such as is found in every dry-goods store, averaging two hundred yards to the spool, is the universal measure. The price charged is more a matter of locality than excellence of workmanship. A certain price will prevail in one section among all quilters there, while in another, not far removed, two or three times that price will be asked for the same work. When many of the old quilts, now treasured as remembrances of our diligent and ambitious ancestors, were made,

ORIGINAL DESIGNS FROM OLD QUILTS

one dollar per spool was the usual price paid for quilting. However, as the number of quilters has decreased, the price of quilting has increased, until as much as five dollars per spool is now asked in some parts of the country. Even at the advanced prices, it is exceedingly difficult to find sufficient quilters to complete the many pieced and appliqué quilts being made.

After the space of some twelve inches, which is as far as the quilter can reach conveniently, has been quilted, the completed portion is rolled up on the side of the frame nearest the quilter. From the other side another section is then unrolled and marked for quilting, and quilted as far as the worker can reach. Thus quilting and rolling are continued until the whole quilt is gone over, after which it is taken from the frame and the edges neatly bound with a narrow piece of bias material, either white or of some harmonizing colour. Since all of the stitches are taken entirely through the quilt, the design worked into the top is repeated on the lining, so that the back makes a white spread of effective pattern in low relief. Very often the back or reverse side is as beautiful as the top, and many lovely quilts have ended their years of service as white counterpanes during that period when the vogue for white beds reigned. Now, however, owners are glad to display them in all their gorgeousness, and they no longer masquerade as white bedspreads.

Occasionally the date of making and the initials of the maker are quilted in a corner, but it is seldom that even this much is visible to tell of the quilt's origin. How interesting it would be if some bits of the story of the maker could have been sewed into a few of the old quilts; for such works of art, that are so long in making, deserve to have some facts relating to them live at least as long as they.

When a bedcover of exceptional warmth is desired, several sheets of cotton or wool prepared for that purpose are laid one over the other between the top and back. As this is too thick to allow a needle to be pushed through easily, and even stitches cannot be taken, then quilting gives way to tying or knotting. Threads of silk, cotton, linen, or wool are drawn through with coarse needles and the ends tied in tight, firm knots. These knots are arranged at close, regular intervals to prevent the interlining from slipping out of place. To this kind of covering is applied the very appro-

FEATHER STAR WITH APPLIQUÉ

The "Feather Star" pieced blocks alternate with blue and white blocks on which are applied scroll designs. This quilt, which is the only one of this pattern, was made about 1835. It was designed by a Mr. Hamill for his sweetheart, Mary Hayward

FIGURE 35

TULIP TREE LEAVES
A modern quilt made by the mountaineers of South Carolina. Colours:
light blue and pink

FIGURE 36

priate name of "comfort." Holland, Germany, Switzerland, and all of Scandinavia use quilted down and feather comforts. In fact, the down comfort has become international in its use. It is found in almost every home in the colder regions of Europe and America, and on chilly nights is a comfort indeed. They are usually made in one colour and, aside from the quilting, which is in bold, artistic designs, are without other decoration. The quilting on down comforts is done by machines made expressly for that work.

Quilting is not confined to the making of quilts. The petticoats worn by the women of Holland are substantial affairs made of either woollen cloth or satin, as the purse permits, heavily interlined and elaborately quilted. The Dutch belle requires from four to nine of these skirts to give her the figure typical of her country. Both the Chinese and Japanese make frequent use of quilting in their thickly padded coats and kimonos, and it may be that from them the early Dutch voyagers and traders brought back the custom to Holland.

A knowledge of the simplest form of sewing is all that is necessary to piece quilts. The running stitch used for narrow seams is the first stitch a

(a) Design from an Old English Quilt [3]   (b) Medallion Design
(c) Pineapple Design

[112]

beginner learns. There are other stitches needed to make a patchwork quilt, which frequently develops into quite an elaborate bit of needlework. The applied designs should always be neatly hemmed to the foundation; some, however, are embroidered and the edges of the designs finished with a buttonhole stitch, and other fancy stitches may be introduced.

In quilt making, as in every other branch of needlework, much experience is required to do good work. It takes much time and practice to acquire accuracy in cutting and arranging all the different pieces. A discriminating eye for harmonizing colours is also a great advantage. But above all requirements the quilt maker must be an expert needleworker, capable of making the multitude of tiny stitches with neatness and precision if she would produce the perfect quilt.

Appreciation of nature is an attribute of many quilt makers, as shown by their efforts to copy various forms of leaf and flower. There are many conventionalized floral patterns on appliqué quilts that give evidence of much ability and originality in their construction. For the pioneer woman there was no convenient school of design, and when she tired of the oft-repeated quilt patterns of her neighbourhood she turned to her garden for suggestions. The striking silhouettes of familiar blossoms seen on many quilts are the direct result of her nature study.

MEXICAN ROSE
Made in 1842.   Colours: red and green.   Note the exquisite quilting

FIGURE 37

CURRANTS AND COCKSCOMB

Small red berries combined with conventionalized leaves. This quilt has
captured first prizes at many state fairs

FIGURE 38

CHAPTER VI

QUILT NAMES

AMONG the most fascinating features of quilt lore are the great number and wonderful variety of names given to quilt designs. A distinct individuality is worked into every quilt by its maker, which in most instances makes it worthy of a name. The many days spent in creating even a simple quilt give the maker ample time in which to ponder over a name for the design, so that the one selected generally reflects some peculiarity in her personality. History, politics, religion, nature, poetry, and romance, all are stitched into the gayly coloured blocks and exert their influence on quilt appellations. Careful consideration of a large number of quilts reveals but few that have been named in a haphazard way; in nearly every instance there was a reason or at least a suggestion for the name.

In most cases the relation between name and design is so evident that the correct name at once suggests itself, even to the novice in quilt making. The common "star" pattern, in which one star is made the centre of each block, is invariably known as the "Five-pointed Star." A variation in the size of the stars or the number of colours entering into their composition has not resulted in any new name.

It is quite usual, however, when there is a slight deviation from a familiar pattern, resulting from either the introduction of some variation or by the omission of a portion of the old design, to make a corresponding change in the name. Good illustrations of this custom are the minor alterations which have been made in the tree trunk of the "tree" pattern. These may be so slight as to be entirely unobserved by the casual admirer, yet they are responsible for at least three new names: "Pine Tree," "Temperance Tree," and "Tree of Paradise." A minor change in the ordinary "Nine Patch," with a new name as a result, is another striking example of how very slight an alteration may be in order to inspire a new title. In this case, the central block is cut somewhat larger than in the old "Nine Patch," and the four corner blocks are, by comparison with the centre block, quite small. This slight change is in reality a magical

CONVENTIONAL APPLIQUÉ

The designs are buttonholed around. Colours: soft green and rose. This quilt is over 100 years old

FIGURE 39

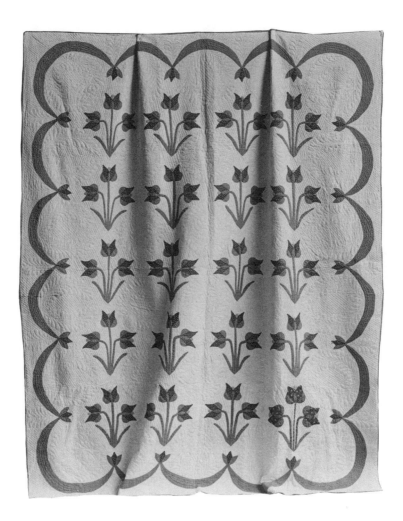

SINGLE TULIP
Colours: red and yellow. Seventy-five years old

FIGURE 40

transformation, for the staid "Nine Patch" has now become a lively "Puss-in-the-Corner." The changes in some patterns have come about through efforts to make a limited amount of highly prized colour brighten a whole quilt. This circumstance, as much as any other, has been the cause of new names.

Important events occurring during the construction periods of old quilts are quite frequently recalled to us by their names. The stirring frontier activities and the great men of history made impressions on the mind of the housewife which found expression in the names of her quilts. "Washington's Plumes," "Mexican Rose," and "Rose of Dixie" are old quilt names reflecting domestic interest in important events. The hardships and vicissitudes endured by the sturdy pioneers were constantly in the minds of the early American quilters and inspired many names. "Pilgrim's Pride," "Bear's Paws," "Rocky Road to Kansas," "Texas Tears," and "Rocky Road to California" have great interest as they reveal to us the thoughts of our great-grandmothers over their quilting frames.

The names having political significance, which were attached to quilts, show that the women as well as the men had a keen interest in the affairs of our country in its earlier days. "Old Tippecanoe," "Lincoln's Platform," "Harrison Rose," "Democrat Rose," "Whig Rose," and "Radical Rose" are all suggestive of the great discussion over slavery. Of the last name, an old lady, famous for her quilt making, said: [1] "Here's my 'Radical Rose.' I reckon you've heard I was the first human that ever put black in a Radical Rose. Thar hit is, right plumb in the middle. Well, whenever you see black in a Radical Rose you can know hit war made atter the second year of the war (Civil War). Hit was this way, ever' man war a-talkin' about the Radicals and all the women tuk to makin' Radical Roses. One day I got to studying that thar ought to be some black in that thar pattern, sence half the trouble was to free the niggers, and hit didn't look fair to leave them out. And from that day to this thar's been black in ever' Radical Rose."

Other names having patriotic, political, or historical significance are:

Union	Star-Spangled Banner
Yankee Puzzle	Confederate Rose
Continental	Boston Puzzle
Union Calico Quilt	

[118]

There is also the "Centennial" in commemoration of the Centennial Exposition held at Philadelphia in 1876, and "The World's Fair," "World's Fair Puzzle," and "World's Fair Blocks" to perpetuate the grandeurs of the great exposition held at Chicago in 1893.

Religion is closely associated with the life of the industrious, sober-minded dwellers of our villages and farms, and it is the most natural thing in the world for the Biblical teachings to crop out in the names of their quilts, as the following names indicate:

Garden of Eden	Solomon's Crown
Golden Gates	Star of Bethlehem
Jacob's Ladder	Tree of Paradise
Joseph's Coat	Forbidden Fruit Tree
Solomon's Temple	

The glories of the sky enjoy ample prominence among quilt names. Beginning with the "Rising Sun," of which there are several different designs, there follow "Sunshine" and "Sunburst," then "Rainbow," and finally a whole constellation of "Stars":

Blazing Star	Chicago Star
Brunswick Star	Columbia Star
Combination Star	Crosses and Stars

Cluster of Stars	Seven Stars
California Star	Star Lane
Diamond Star	Star of Bethlehem
Eight-pointed Star	Star and Chains
Evening Star	Star of Many Points
Feather Star	Star and Squares
Five-pointed Star	Star and Cubes
Flying Star	Star Puzzle
Four X Star	Shooting Star
Four Stars Patch	Star of the West
Joining Star	Star and Cross
Ladies' Beautiful Star	Star of Texas
Morning Star	Stars upon Stars
New Star	Squares and Stars
Novel Star	St. Louis Star
Odd Star	Star A
Premium Star	Twinkling Star
Ribbon Star	Union Star
Rolling Star	Wheel and Star
Sashed Star	Western Star

In connection with the "Star" quilt names it is worthy of notice that geometric names outnumber those of any other class. "Squares," "triangles," and "circles" are well represented, but the "Stars" easily lead with nearly fifty names.

Names of various other geometric patterns appear below:

Art Square	Beggar's Blocks
Barrister's Blocks	Box Blocks

Circle within Circle	Memory Circle
Cross within Cross	New Four Patch
Cross and Crown	New Nine Patch
Cube Work	Octagon
Cube Lattice	Pinwheel Square
Diamonds	Red Cross
Diamond Cube	Ribbon Squares
Diamond Design	Roman Cross
Double Squares	Sawtooth Patchwork
Domino and Square	Square and Swallow
Eight-point Design	Square and a Half
Five Stripes	Squares and Stripes
Fool's Square	Square and Triangle
Four Points	Stripe Squares
Greek Cross	The Cross
Greek Square	The Diamond
Hexagonal	Triangle Puzzle
Interlaced Blocks	Triangular Triangle
Maltese Cross	Variegated Diamonds
Memory Blocks	Variegated Hexagons

Names of a nautical turn are to be expected for quilts which originate in seaside cottages and seaport villages. "Bounding Betty," "Ocean Waves," and "Storm at Sea" have a flavour as salty as the spray which dampens them when they are spread out to sun by the sandy shore.

That poetry and romance have left their mark on the quilt is shown by the names that have been drawn from these sources. "Lady of the Lake,"

"Charm," "Air Castle," "Wheel of Fortune," and "Wonder of the World" are typical examples. Sentimental names are also in evidence, as "Love Rose," "Lovers' Links," "True Lovers' Knot," "Friendship Quilt," and "Wedding Knot."

Nature furnishes more suggestions for beautiful quilt designs than any other source. So frequently are her models resorted to by quilt makers the world over that many different designs have been inspired by the same leaf or flower. The rose especially is used again and again, and will always be the favourite flower of the quilter. There are at least twenty "rose" names to prove how this flower has endeared itself to the devotees of piece-block and quilting frame:

Rose	Prairie Rose
California Rose	Rose of Sharon
Complex Rose	Rose of Dixie
Confederate Rose	Rose of the Carolinas
Democrat Rose	Rosebud and Leaves
Dutch Rose	Rose Album
Harrison Rose	Rose of Le Moine
Harvest Rose	Radical Rose
Love Rose	Whig Rose
Mexican Rose	Wild Rose

Wreath of Roses

OHIO ROSE

This "Rose" quilt was made in Ohio about 80 years ago.   Colours: red,
pink, and two shades of green

FIGURE 41

ROSE OF SHARON

Made in Indiana about 65 years ago. It has a wool interlining instead of
the usual cotton

FIGURE 42

Other flowery names are also popular:

Basket of Lilies	Morning Glory
Bouquet	Morning Gray Wreath
Cleveland Lilies	Persian Palm Lily
Cactus Blossom	Poppy
Chrysanthemums	Pansies and Butterflies
Double Peony	Single Sunflowers
Daisies	Sunflowers
Daffodils and Butterflies	Tulip in Vase
Field Daisies	Tassel Plant
Flower Basket	Tulip Blocks
Iris	Three-flowered Sunflower
Jonquils	The Mayflower
Lily Quilt Pattern	Tulip Lady Finger
Lily of the Valley	White Day Lily

When seeking flowers that lend themselves readily to quilt designs it is best to choose those whose leaves and blossoms present clear, distinct, and easily traced outlines. The names of many of the quaint varieties that flourish in old-fashioned gardens, as lilacs, phlox, larkspur, and marigolds, are absent from the list. This is because their lacy foliage and complex arrangement of petals cannot be reproduced satisfactorily in quilt materials.

Even the lowly vegetables secure some mention among quilt names with "Corn and Beans." The fruits and trees are well represented, as noted by the following list:

Apple Hexagon	May Berry Leaf
Cherry Basket	Olive Branch
California Oak Leaf	Orange Peel
Cypress Leaf	Oak Leaf and Tulip
Christmas Tree	Oak Leaf and Acorns
Fruit Basket	Pineapple
Grape Basket	Pine Tree
Hickory Leaf	Sweet Gum Leaf
Imperial Tea	Strawberry
Indian Plum	Tea Leaf
Live Oak Tree	Tufted Cherry
Little Beech Tree	Temperance Tree
Maple Leaf	Tulip Tree Leaves

The names of birds and insects are almost as popular as those of flowers, as this list will bear witness:

Bluebird	Goose in the Pond
Brown-tailed Moth	Honeycomb
Butterflies	Honeycomb Patch
Bird's Nest	Hen and Chickens
Crow's Foot	King's Crows
Chimney Swallows	Peacocks and Flowers
Cockscomb	Spider's Den
Dove in the Window	Shoo Fly
Duck and Ducklings	Spider's Web
Four Little Birds	Swarm of Bees
Goose Tracks	The Two Doves

Wild Goose Chase

[124]

ORIGINAL FLORAL DESIGNS

This quilt contains twenty blocks, each of a different design. The border
is composed of festoons decorated with cockscomb and sprays of
flowers. A southern Indiana quilt made about 1825

FIGURE 43

CONVENTIONAL TULIP
Made from a pattern used 130 years ago. Colours: pink and green

FIGURE 44

The animals also must be credited with their share of names:

Bear's Foot	Four Frogs Quilt
Bear's Paws	Leap Frog
Bat's Wings	Puss in the Corner
Bunnies	The Snail's Trail
Cats and Mice	Toad in the Puddle
Flying Bat	The Lobster (1812)

Occasionally the quilt maker was honoured by having her name given to her handiwork, as " Mrs. Morgan's Choice," "Mollie's Choice," "Sarah's Favourite," and "Fanny's Fan." Aunts and grandmothers figure as prominently in the naming of quilts as they do in the making of them. "Aunt Sukey's Patch," "Aunt Eliza's Star Point," " Grandmother's Own," "Grandmother's Dream," and "Grandmother's Choice" are typical examples.

Quilt names in which reference is made to persons and personalities are quite numerous, as is proved by the list given below:

Coxey's Camp	Handy Andy
Crazy Ann	Hands All Around
Dutchman's Puzzle	Hobson's Kiss
Everybody's Favourite	Indian Plumes
Eight Hands Around	Indian Hatchet
Grandmother's Choice	Jack's House
Garfield's Monument	Joseph's Necktie
Gentleman's Fancy	King's Crown

[125]

Lady Fingers	Sister's Choice
Ladies' Wreath	The Tumbler
Ladies' Delight	The Hand
Mary's Garden	The Priscilla
Mrs. Cleveland's Choice	Twin Sisters
Old Maid's Puzzle	Vice-president's Quilt
Odd Fellows' Chain	Widower's Choice
Princess Feather	Washington's Puzzle
President's Quilt	Washington's Sidewalk

Washington's Plumes

Names derived both from local neighbourhoods and foreign lands occupy a prominent place in the quilt list:

Arabic Lattice	Philadelphia Beauty
American Log Patch	Philadelphia Pavement
Arkansas Traveller	Rocky Glen
Alabama Beauty	Royal Japanese Vase
Blackford's Beauty	Rocky Road to Kansas
Boston Puzzle	Rocky Road to California
Columbian Puzzle	Road to California
Cross Roads to Texas	Roman Stripe
Double Irish Chain	Rockingham's Beauty
French Basket	Rose of Dixie
Grecian Design	Rose of the Carolinas
Indiana Wreath	Star of Texas
Irish Puzzle	Texas Flower
Kansas Troubles	The Philippines
Linton	Texas Tears
London Roads	Venetian Design
Mexican Rose	Village Church
Oklahoma Boomer	Virginia Gentleman

Sometimes the names of a flower and a locality are combined, as in "Persian Palm Lily" and "Carolina Lily." This latter design is quite a popular one in the Middle West, where it is known also as "Star Flower."

Figures and letters come in for some attention, for a few of the designs thus named are quite artistic. The best known are "Boxed I's," "Capital I," "Double Z," "Four E's," "Fleur-de-Lis," "Letter H," "Letter X," and "T Quartette."

Inanimate objects, particularly those about the house, inspired many names for patterns, some of which are quite appropriate. A number of such names are given here:

Album	Flutter Wheel
Base Ball	Fan
Basket Quilt	Fan Patch
Block Album	Fan and Rainbow
Brickwork Quilt	Ferris Wheel
Carpenter's Rule	Flower Pot
Carpenter's Square	Hour Glass
Churn Dash	Ice Cream Bowl
Cog Wheel	Log Patch
Compass	Log Cabin
Crossed Canoes	Necktie
Diagonal Log Chain	Needle Book
Domino	New Album
Double Wrench	Pincushion and Burr

Paving Blocks	Spools
Pickle Dish	Shield
Rolling Pinwheel	Scissor's Chain
Rolling Stone	Square Log Cabin
Sashed Album	The Railroad
Shelf Chain	The Disk
Snowflake	The Globe
Snowball	The Wheel
Stone Wall	Tile Patchwork
Sugar Loaf	Watered Ribbon

Wind Mill

Occasionally the wag of the family had his opportunity, for it took some one with a strain of dry humour to suggest "Old Bachelor's Puzzle," "Drunkard's Path," and "All Tangled Up," or to have ironically called one quilt a "Blind Man's Fancy."

Imagination was not lacking when it came to applying apt names to some of the simplest designs. To have called rows of small triangles running diagonally across a quilt the "Wild Goose Chase," the maker must have known something of the habits of wild geese, for as these migrate from North to South and back again following the summer's warmth, they fly one behind the other in long V-shaped lines. The resemblance of these lines, swiftly moving across the sky, to her neat

[128]

CONVENTIONAL ROSE

A very striking pattern, made in Indiana about 75 years ago.   Colours:
red, pink, and green

FIGURE 45

CONVENTIONAL ROSE WREATH

This "Wreath of Roses" design has been in use for over 100 years.
Colours: red, green, pink, and yellow

FIGURE 46

rows of triangles supplied the quilt maker with her inspiration.

Names that are grotesque, or fanciful, or so descriptive that their mention is sure to provoke a grin, occur with pleasing frequency. Who can help but smile at "Hairpin Catcher," "Hearts and Gizzards," or "Tangled Garters?" Other grotesque names worthy of mention are:

An Odd Pattern	No Name Quilt
Autograph Quilt	Pullman Puzzle
Boy's Nonsense	Puzzle File
Brick Pile	Robbing Peter to Pay Paul
Broken Dish	State House Steps
Cake Stand	Steps to the Altar
Crazy Quilt	Swing in the Centre
Devil's Puzzle	The X quisite
Fantastic Patch	Tick-Tack-Toe
Fool's Puzzle	Vestibule

The everyday quilts, not particularly beautiful, perhaps, but nevertheless so essential to the family comfort, are also considered worthy of names. Homely and prosaic as their owners, the following names have a peculiar rugged quality entirely lacking in the fanciful ones given to their more artistic sisters:

[129]

An Old Patchwork

Bedtime

Coarse Woven Patch

Country Farm

Crib Quilt

Crosses and Losses

Economy

Home Treasure

Odds and Ends

Odd Patchwork

Old Scrap Patchwork

Right and Left

Simple Design

Swinging Corners

The Old Homestead

Twist and Turn

Twist Patchwork

Winding Walk

Workbox

In the old days grown-up folks were not the only ones who had to do with naming the quilts; children shared in the honour, and many of the quaint and fantastic names were the result of humouring their fancies. There was no "B'rer Rabbit" in quilt lore, but he was not missed when the two or three youngsters who cuddled in the old-fashioned trundle bed could have so many other fascinating names for their quilts. "Four Little Birds," "Ducks and Ducklings," "Children's Delight," "The Little Red House," "Goose in the Pond," "The House That Jack Built," "Toad in the Puddle," and "Johnny Around the Corner" are some of the old names still in use to-day. Any one of these patterns made up into a quilt was a treasure to imaginative children, and it was doubly so when they could pick out among the tiny blocks bits of colour

[130]

that were once in their own gay dresses and pina-
fores.

Clinging lavender wisteria, sweet jasmine, and
even scarlet amarylis pale beside the glowing
colours displayed during sunny spring days on the
gallery rails of many country homes through Dela-
ware and Virginia. These picturesque scenes, in
which the familiar domestic art supplies the essential touch of colour, are aptly described by
Robert and Elizabeth Shackleton, those indefatigable searchers for the beautiful among the relics of
our forefathers. [2]

"In many a little village, and in many an isolated
mountain home, the old-time art of making patchwork coverlets is remembered and practised. Some
may be found that are generations old; others are
new, but made in precisely the old-time way, and
after the same patterns. Many are in gorgeous
colours, in glowing yellows, greens, and purples;
and being a matter of housewifely pride, they are
often thrown over the 'gallery rail' so their glory
may be seen.

"One guest bed had nineteen quilts! Not to
sleep under such a padded mountain, but it was
the most natural method of display. Each quilt

had its name. There was the "Western Star," the "Rose of the Carolinas," the "Log Cabin," the "Virginia Gentleman," the "Fruit Basket," the "Lily of the Valley"—as many special names as there are designs."

POINSETTIA
An appliqué quilt of red, blue, and green

FIGURE 47

WHIG ROSE

On the reverse side is a small "gold pocket" in which valuables may be
secreted.   Colours: yellow, red, and green

FIGURE 48

CHAPTER VII

QUILT COLLECTIONS AND EXHIBITIONS

IN SPITE of their wide distribution and vast quantity, the number of quilts readily accessible to those who are interested in them is exceedingly small. This is particularly true of those quilts which possess artistic merit and historic interest, and a considerable amount of inquiry is sometimes necessary in order to bring forth even a single quilt of more than ordinary beauty. It is unfortunate for this most useful and pleasant art that its masterpieces are so shy and loath to display their charms, for it is mainly from the rivalry induced by constant display that all arts secure their best stimulus. However, some very remarkable achievements in quilting have been brought to light from time to time, to the great benefit of this best of household arts.

There is in existence to-day no complete collection of quilts readily available to the public at large. No museum in this country or abroad has a collection worthy of the name, the nearest approach to it being in the great South Kensington Museum in London.[1] While many institutions possess one or more specimens, these have been preserved more often on account of some historic association than because of exceptional beauty or artistic merit. It is only in the rare instance of a family collection, resulting from the slow accumulation by more than one generation of quilt enthusiasts, that a quilt collection at all worth while can be found. In such a case the owner is generally so reticent concerning his treasures that the community as a whole is never given the opportunity to profit by them.

In families where accumulations have reached the dignity in numbers that will justify being called collections, the quilts belonging to different branches of the family have been passed along from one generation to another, until they have become the property of one person. Among collections of this sort are found many rare and beautiful quilts, as only the best and choicest of all that were made have been preserved. There are also occasional large collections of quilts that are the work of one industrious maker who has spent the greater portion of her life piecing and quilting. The Kentucky mountain woman who had "eighty-three, all different, and all her own makin'," is a typical example of this class.[2]

The vastness of their numbers and the great extent of their everyday use serve to check the collecting of quilts. As a whole, quilts are extremely heterogeneous and democratic; they are made so generally over the whole country that no distinct types have been developed, and they are possessed so universally that there is little social prestige to be gained by owning an uncommonly large number. Consequently even the most ardent quilt lovers are usually satisfied when they possess enough for their own domestic needs, with perhaps a few extra for display in the guest chambers.

Much of the social pleasure of the pioneer women was due to their widespread interest in quilts. Aside from the quilting bees, which were notable affairs, collecting quilt patterns was to many women a source of both interest and enjoyment. Even the most ambitious woman could not hope to make a quilt like every design which she admired, so, to appease the desire for the numerous ones she

[135]

was unable to make, their patterns were collected. These collections of quilt patterns—often quite extensive, frequently included single blocks of both pieced and patched designs. There was always a neighbourly and friendly interest taken in such collections, as popular designs were exchanged and copied many times. Choice remnants of prints and calicoes were also shared with the neighbours. Occasionally from trunks or boxes, long hidden in dusty attics, some of these old blocks come to light, yellowed with age and frayed at the edges, to remind us of the simple pleasures of our grandmothers.

At the present time there is a marked revival of interest in quilts and their making. The evidences of this revival are the increasing demand for competent quilters, the desire for new quilt patterns, and the growing popularity of quilt exhibitions. Concerning exhibits of quilts, there is apparent—at least in the northern part of the United States—a noticeable increase in popular appreciation of those held at county and state fairs. This is a particularly fortunate circumstance for the development of the art, because the county fair, "our one steadfast institution in a world of change," is so intimately connected with the lives and is so dear to the hearts of our people.

In addition to the pleasures and social diversions which that annual rural festival—the county fair—affords, it is an educational force that is not sufficiently appreciated by those who live beyond the reach of its spell. At best, country life contains long stretches of monotony, and any interest with which it can be relieved is a most welcome addition to the lives of the women in rural communities. At the fair women are touched to new thoughts on common themes. They come to meet each other and talk over the latest kinks in jelly making, the progress of their children, and similar details of their family affairs. They come to get standards of living and to gather ideas of home decoration and entertainment for the long evenings when intercourse, even with the neighbours, becomes infrequent.

There is not the least doubt concerning the beneficial influence of the local annual fair on the life of the adjacent neighbourhood. At such a fair the presence of a varied and well-arranged display of needlework, which has been produced by the womenfolk, is of the greatest assistance in making

[137]

the community one in which it is worth while to live. Not only does it serve as a stimulus to those who look forward to the fair and put into their art the very best of their ability in order that they may surpass their competitor next door, but it also serves as an inspiration to those who are denied the faculty of creating original designs, yet nevertheless take keen pleasure in the production of beautiful needlework. It is to this latter class that an exhibition of quilts is of real value, because it provides them with new patterns that can be applied to the quilts which must be made. With fresh ideas for their inspiration, work which would otherwise be tedious becomes a real pleasure.

For the women of the farm the exhibit of domestic arts and products occupies the preëminent place at the county fair. In this exhibit the display of patchwork is sure to arouse the liveliest enthusiasm. A visitor at a fair in a western state very neatly describes this appreciation shown to quilts: "We used to hear a great deal about the sad and lonely fate of the western farmer's wife, but there was little evidence of loneliness in the appearance of these women who surrounded the quilts and fancywork in the Domestic Arts Building."

HARRISON ROSE

This quilt is at least 75 years old. The rose is pieced of old rose and two
shades of pink; the stem and leaves are appliqué

FIGURE 49

DETAIL OF HARRISON ROSE, SHOWING QUILTING

FIGURE 50

In connection with the display of needlework at rural fairs, it is interesting to note how ancient is this custom. In the "Social History of Ancient Ireland" is the following description of an Irish fair held during the fourth century—long before the advent of St. Patrick and Christianity: "The people of Leinster every three years during the first week of August held the 'Fair of Carman.' Great ceremony and formality attended this event, the King of Leinster and his court officiating. Music formed a prominent part of the amusement. One day was set apart for recitation of poems and romantic tales, another for horse and chariot racing. In another part of the Fair people indulged in uproarious fun, crowded around showmen, jugglers, clowns with painted faces or hideously grotesqued masks. Prizes publicly presented by King or dignitary were given to winners of various contests. Needlework was represented by 'the slope of the embroidering women,' where women actually did their work in the presence of spectators." [3]

A very important factor in the recent revival of interest in quilts has been the springing up of impromptu exhibits as "benefits" for worthy causes, the raising of funds for which is a matter of popular

[139]

interest. Does a church need a new roof, a hospital some more furnishings, or a college a new building? And have all the usual methods of raising money become hackneyed and uninspiring to those interested in furthering the project? To those confronted with such a money-raising problem the quilt exhibition offers a most welcome solution. For not only does such an exhibition offer a new form of entertainment, but it also has sources of interesting material from which to draw that are far richer than commonly supposed.

Not so very long ago "The Country Contributor" undertook the task of giving a quilt show, and her description of it is distinctly worth while: [4]

"My ideas were a bit vague. I had a mental picture of some beautiful quilts I knew of hung against a wall somewhere for people to come and look at and wonder over. So we announced the quilt show and then went on our way rejoicing. A good-natured school board allowed us to have the auditorium at the high school building for the display and the quilt agitation began.

"A day or two before the show, which was to be on a Saturday, it began to dawn upon me that I might be buried under an avalanche of quilts.

The old ones were terribly large. They were made to cover a fat feather bed or two and to hang down to hide the trundle bed underneath, and, though the interlining of cotton was very thin and even, still the weight of a quilt made by one's grandmother is considerable.

"We betook ourselves to the school building at an early hour on Saturday morning and the fun began. We were to receive entries until one o'clock, when the exhibition was to begin.

"In looking back now at this little event, I wonder we could have been so benighted as to imagine we could do it in a day! After about an hour, during which the quilts came in by the dozen, I sent in a general alarm to friends and kindred for help. We engaged a carpenter, strung up wires and ropes, and by some magic of desperation we got those quilts on display, 118 of them, by one o'clock.

"One lovely feature of this quilt show was the reverence with which men brought to us the quilts their mothers made. Plain farmers, busy workers, retired business men, came to us, their faces softened to tenderness, handed us, with mingled pride and devotion, their big bundle containing a contribution to the display, saying in softened accents, 'My mother made it.' And each and every quilt brought thus was worthy of a price on its real merit—not for its hallowed association alone.

"Time and space would fail if I should try to tell about the quilts that came in at our call for an exhibition. There were so many prize quilts (fully two thirds of the quilts entered deserved prizes) that it is difficult to say what finally decided the blue ribbon. However, the quilt which finally carried it away was fairly typical of those of the early part of the nineteenth century. A rose pattern was applied in coloured calicoes on each alternate block. The geometrical calculation, the miraculous neatness of this work, can scarcely be exaggerated. But this is not the wonder of the thing. The real wonder is the quilting. This consisted in copying the design, petal for petal, leaf for leaf, in needlework upon every alternate block of white muslin. How these workers accomplished the raised designs on plain white muslin is the mystery. How raised flowers, leaves, plumes, baskets, bunches of fruit, even animal and bird shapes, could be shown in bas-relief on these quilt blocks without hopelessly 'puckering' the material, none of us can imagine."

No other inspiration that can equal our fairs has been offered to the quilters of our day. Public recognition of good work and the premiums which accompany this recognition augment the desire to excell in the art of quilt making. The keen competition engendered results in the most exact and painstaking work possible being put upon quilts that are entered for the "blue ribbon." The materials, designs, and colours chosen for these quilts are given the most careful consideration, and the stitchery is as nearly perfect as it is possible to make it.

Some of the finest old quilts that have been preserved are repeatedly exhibited at county and state fairs, and have more than held their own with those made in recent years. One shown at an exhibition of quilts and coverlets, held in a city in southern Indiana in 1914, had been awarded the first premium at thirty-seven different fairs. This renowned and venerable quilt had been made more than seventy-five years before. Its design is the familiar one known as the "Rose of Sharon"; both the needlework on the design and the quilting are exquisite, the stitches being all but invisible.

A striking instance of the influence of fairs upon quilt making is shown in the number of beautiful quilts that have been made expressly for display in exhibitions at state fairs in the Middle West. One such collection, worthy of special notice, consists of seven quilts: three of elaborate designs in patchwork and four made up of infinitesimal pieces. Every stitch, both on the handsome tops and in the perfect quilting, was wrought with careful patience by an oldtime quilt maker. The aggregate amount of stitching upon these seven quilts seems enough to constitute the work of a lifetime. The material in these quilts, except one which is of silk, is fine white muslin and the reliable coloured calicoes of fifty years ago.

This extraordinary and beautiful collection is now being carefully preserved by an appreciative daughter, who tells how it was possible for her mother to accomplish this great task of needlework. The maker was the wife of a busy and prosperous farmer of northern Indiana. As on all farms in that region during the pioneer days, the home was the centre of manufacture of those

ORIGINAL ROSE DESIGN MADE IN 1840

The maker was lame, and only able to walk about in her garden. Colours:
red, green, pink, and yellow

FIGURE 51

PINEAPPLE DESIGN
Colours: red and green

FIGURE 52

various articles necessary to the welfare and comfort of the family. This indulgent farmer, realizing that his wife's quilt making was work of a higher plane than routine housekeeping, employed two stout daughters of a less fortunate neighbour to relieve her of the heavier household duties. Such work that required her direct supervision, as jelly making and fruit canning, was done in the evenings. This allowed the ambitious little woman ample time to pursue her art during the bright clear hours of daylight.

Belonging to the collections of individuals are many old quilts which possess more than ordinary interest, not so much on account of their beauty or unusual patterns, but because of their connection with some notable personage or historic event. The number of quilts which are never used, but which are most carefully treasured by their owners on account of some sentimental or historic association, is far greater than generally supposed. While most of the old quilts so jealously hidden in closet and linen chest have no extraordinary beauty, yet from time to time there comes into notice one which possesses—in addition to its interesting connection with the past—an exquisite and mellow beauty which only tasteful design enhanced by age can give.

Quite often beautiful quilts are found in old trunks and bureaus, which have gathered dust for untold years in attics and storerooms. Opportunities to ransack old garrets are greatly appreciated by collectors, as the uncertainty of what may be found gives zest to their search. It was of such old treasure trove that the hangings were found to make what Harriet Beecher Stowe in her novel, "The Minister's Wooing," calls "the garret boudoir." This was a cozy little enclosure made by hanging up old quilts, blankets, and coverlets so as to close off one corner of the garret. Her description of an old quilt used in this connection is especially interesting. It "was a bed quilt pieced in tiny blocks, none of them bigger than a sixpence, containing, as Mrs. Katy said, pieces of the gowns of all her grandmothers, aunts, cousins, and female relatives for years back; and mated to it was one of the blankets which had served Mrs. Scudder's uncle in his bivouac at Valley Forge." [5]

To view the real impromptu exhibitions of quilts—for which, by the way, no admission fee is charged—one should drive along any country road on a bright sunny day in early spring. It is at this time that the household bedding is given its annual airing, and consequently long lines hung with quilts are frequent and interesting sights. During this periodical airing there becomes apparent a seemingly close alliance between patchwork and nature, as upon the soft green background of new leaves the beauty of the quilts is thrown into greater prominence. All the colours of the rainbow can be seen in the many varieties of design, for there is not a line that does not bear a startling "Lone Star of Texas," "Rising Sun," or some equally attractive pattern. Gentle breezes stir the quilts so that their designs and colours gain in beauty as they slowly wave to and fro. When the apple, cherry, and peach trees put on their new spring dresses of delicate blossoms and stand in graceful groups in the background, then the picture becomes even more charming.

This periodical airing spreads from neighbour to neighbour, and as one sunny day follows another all the clothes lines become weighted with burdens of brightest hues. Of course, there is no rivalry between owners, or no unworthy desire to show off,

[147]

yet, have you ever seen a line full of quilts hung wrong side out? It has been suggested that at an exhibition is the logical place to see quilts bloom. Yet, while it is a rare chance to see quilts of all kinds and in all states of preservation, yet it is much like massing our wild Sweet Williams, Spring Beauties, and Violets in a crowded greenhouse. They bravely do their best, but you can fairly see them gasping for the fresh, free air of their woodland homes. A quilt hung on a clothes line in the dooryard and idly flapping in the wind receives twice the appreciation given one which is sedately folded across a wire with many others in a crowded, jealous row.

"PINK ROSE" DESIGN

PLATE 1

THE IRIS DESIGN

In this design the iris has been conventionalized so as to make it consistent
with its natural growth—the flowers stretching up in a stately
array beyond their long-pointed leaves

PLATE 2

THE "SNOWFLAKE" QUILT DESIGN

Brings to one's imagination the sharp-pointed, glistening snowflakes against a background of blue sky. The quilting in fine stitches simulates the applied pattern, and the border suggests drifts of snow as one sees them after a winter's storm

PLATE 3

THE "WIND-BLOWN TULIP" DESIGN
Seems to bring a breath of springtime both in form and colour. Even the border flowers seem to be waving and nodding in the breeze

PLATE 4

POPPY DESIGN

This is applied patchwork and therefore much more easily made than pieced
work; very simple quilting gives prominence to the design

PLATE 5

MORNING GLORIES
In one of their many beautiful and delicate varieties were chosen for this
quilt, and while the design is conventional to a certain extent
it shows the natural grace of the growing vine

PLATE 6

THE DOGWOOD QUILT

Offers another choice in flower designs. The full-grown blossoms on the
green background remind us of the beauty of trees
and flowers in early spring

PLATE 7

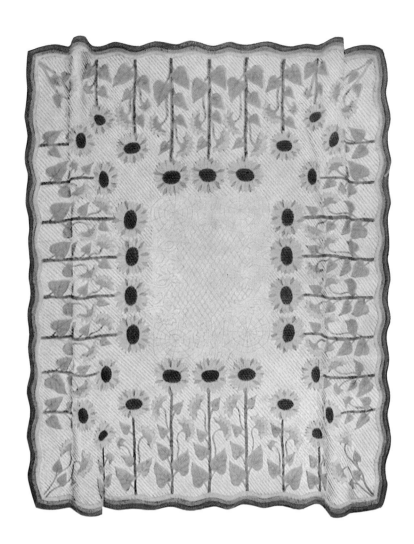

THE SUNFLOWER QUILT

Shows a realistic, bold design of vivid colouring. The border is harmonious, suggesting a firm foundation for the stems. The quilting in the centre is a design of spider webs, leaves, and flowers

PLATE 8

AS GOLDEN BUTTERFLIES AND PANSIES

Are so often playmates of little ones in the garden, and beloved by them,
they were chosen for the motifs of this child's quilt

PLATE 9

"KEEPSAKE QUILT"

The sunbonnet lassies suggest an outing or a call from playmates on the morrow. These lassies may be dressed in bits of the gowns of the little maid, and the quilt thus become a "keepsake quilt"

PLATE 10

THE WILD ROSE

That loves to grow in fragrant, tangled masses by the roadside was made to
march in prim rows on this child's quilt

PLATE 11

DAISY QUILT
For a child's bed

PLATE 12

MORNING GLORY

It must be "early to bed and early to rise" for the child who would see the
sweet morning glory in all its loveliness, as it must be
found before all the dew is gone

PLATE 13

THE BEDTIME QUILT

With its procession of night-clad children will be excellent "company" for
a tot, to whom a story may be told of the birds that sleep in the
little trees while the friendly stars keep watch

PLATE 14

THE NEW PATCHWORK CUSHIONS

Marie Webster's original designs for appliqué cushions appeared on this full color page in the August 1911 issue of *The Ladies' Home Journal*.

PLATE 15

GRAPES AND VINES

Marie Webster finished this quilt in 1914, just in time for its photograph to be included in her book. (See Figure 66.) 74 x 74 inches. (© 1989, Indianapolis Museum of Art. Gift of Mrs. Gerrish Thurber)

PLATE 16

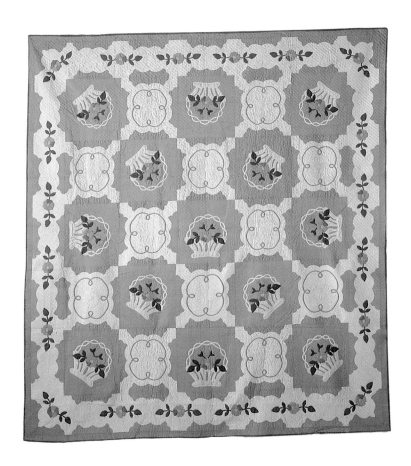

FRENCH BASKETS WITH ROSES

A variation on Marie Webster's 1914 design, French Baskets with Daisies. Her younger sister, Emma Daugherty, made this quilt in 1930. 82 x 92 inches. (Collection of Katherine Webster Dwight)

PLATE 17

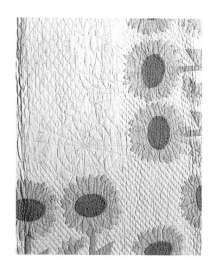

SUNFLOWER—DETAIL
This is a detail of the quilt shown in Plate 8, which was first published in the January 1912 issue of *The Ladies' Home Journal.* (© 1989, Indianapolis Museum of Art. Gift of Mrs. Gerrish Thurber)

PLATE 18

THE BUNNIES
PATTERN
A blueprint and colored tissue paper mock-up were included in Marie Webster's pattern packet, which sold for 50 cents. The quilt was made in 1929 by a friend of the Websters. (Matter Family Collection)

PLATE 19

BUNNIES
Marie Webster designed the Bunnies pattern in 1914 and stitched this example when she was 80 years old, as a gift for her grand-daughter. 41 x 60 inches. (Collection of Rosalind Webster Perry)

PLATE 20

WREATH OF ROSES

In October 1915, *The Ladies' Home Journal* published this Marie Webster version of a traditional favorite. A detail of this quilt, made in 1930, appears in Plate 27. 80 x 94 inches. (Collection of Rosalind Webster Perry)

PLATE 21

POINSETTIA

A stunning color combination and a diagonal set distinguish this quilt, which Marie Webster designed and made in 1917. 62 x 94 inches. (© 1989, Indianapolis Museum of Art. Gift of Mrs. Gerrish Thurber)

PLATE 22

NASTURTIUM WREATH

Inspired by the flowers in her garden, Marie Webster designed this
exuberant pattern in the early 1920s. The quilt was made in 1930.
78 x 89 inches. (Collection of Katherine Webster Dwight)

PLATE 23

PRIMROSE WREATH

Traditional feather wreath quilting enhances the beauty of this colorful quilt, designed by Marie Webster about 1925. 62 x 92 inches.
(© 1989, Indianapolis Museum of Art. Gift of Mrs. Gerrish Thurber)

PLATE 24

PINK DOGWOOD IN BASKETS
The Ladies' Home Journal offered a pattern for this popular Marie Webster design in September 1927. 83 x 83 inches. (Collection of Mrs. Gerrish Thurber)

PLATE 25

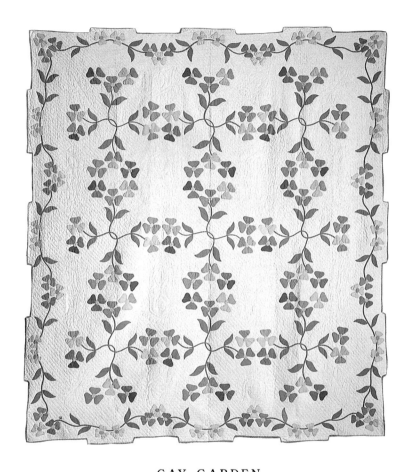

GAY GARDEN

This was one of Marie Webster's last designs and dates from the late 1920s, when she was using a brighter palette of solid color cottons for her appliqué flowers. 78 x 89 inches. (Collection of Rosamond S. Eliassen)

PLATE 26

WREATH OF ROSES DETAIL
This detail of the quilt pictured in Plate 21 shows how Marie Webster constructed her realistic flowers from layers of petals, then outlined them with quilting stitches for a three-dimensional effect.

PLATE 27

RAINBOW — DETAIL
Vibrant new color combinations mark Marie Webster's designs from the 1920s. The whole quilt is shown in Plate 29.

PLATE 28

RAINBOW

An Art Deco-inspired border enhances this design from the mid-1920s. The quilt is one of a pair Marie Webster made for her son and daughter-in-law in 1936. 68 x 93 inches. (Collection of Mrs. Gerrish Thurber)

PLATE 29

INDIANA WREATH

Marie Webster called this appliqué masterpiece from Hartford City, Indiana, "the very perfection of quiltmaking." It was made by Elizabeth J. Hart, who quilted "E. J. Hart, July 1858" underneath the wreath. 88 x 88 inches. (Collection of Mr. and Mrs. Herbert B. Feldmann)

PLATE 30

INDIANA WREATH DETAIL

This detail of the quilt in Plate 30 shows the tiny appliqué pieces and minute quilting stitches which make this such a magnificent work of art.

PLATE 31

NORTH CAROLINA LILY DETAIL

Illustrated in black and white in Figure 34, this quilt belonged to Marie Webster's grandmother, Elizabeth K. Daugherty, whose two daughters, Jennie and Letty, are believed to have made it about 1860. (Collection of Rosalind Webster Perry)

PLATE 32

ORIGINAL FLORAL DESIGNS

This delightful quilt, with its colorful birds and flowers, is also
shown in Figure 43. It was appliquéd in 1844 by Mrs. McCasson and
is now in a museum collection in Terre Haute, Indiana. 78 x 90
inches. (Courtesy of the Vigo County Historical Society)

PLATE 33

WHIG ROSE OR PUMPKIN BLOSSOM

Although captioned "Whig Rose" in this book (Fig. 48), it was called "Pumpkin Blossom" when Emma B. Hodge gave it to the Art Institute of Chicago. It is an early example of machine quilting, made in Michigan about 1848. 76 x 82 inches. (Courtesy of the Art Institute of Chicago, © 1990)

PLATE 34

SINGLE TULIP DETAIL

The quilt from which this detail is taken appears in black and white in Figure 40. The flowers were pieced from printed calicoes, while the leaves, stems and border swags were appliquéd. (Matter Family Collection)

PLATE 35

ORIGINAL ROSE DESIGN

This quilt, also shown in Figure 51, was made by Mary Elizabeth Secrist Ammons, whose family settled in Marion, Indiana, before the Civil War. It was later passed down to her daughter, Elma Ammons Campbell, a friend of Marie Webster. (Collection of Mrs. John O. Campbell)

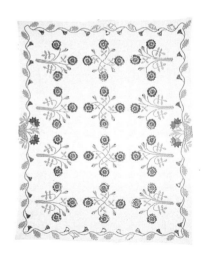

PLATE 36

CHAPTER VIII

THE QUILT'S PLACE IN AMERICAN HOMES

THE dominant characteristics of quilt making are companionship and concentrated interest. Both of these qualities, or—better yet—virtues, must be in evidence in order to bring a quilt to successful completion. The sociable, gossipy "quilting bee," where the quilt is put together and quilted, has planted in every community in which it is an institution the seeds of numberless lifelong friendships. These friendships are being made over the quilting frames to-day just as they were in the pioneer times when a "quilting" was almost the only social diversion. Content with life, fixity of purpose, development of individuality, all are brought forth in every woman who plans and pieces a quilt. The reward of her work lies, not only in the pleasure of doing, but also in the joy of possession—which can be passed on even to future generations, for a well-made quilt is a lasting treasure.

All this is quite apart from the strictly useful functions which quilts perform so creditably in every home, for quilts are useful as well as artistic. In summer nights they are the ideal emergency covering for the cool hour before dawn, or after a rapid drop in temperature, caused by a passing thunderstorm. But in the long chill nights of winter, when the snow sifts in through the partly raised window and all mankind snuggles deeper into the bed clothes, then all quilts may be truly said to do their duty. And right well they do it, too, as all those who love to linger within their cozy shelter on frosty December mornings will testify.

As a promoter of good-will and neighbourly interest during the times when our new country was being settled, and woman's social intercourse was very limited, the "quilting bee" holds a worthy place close beside the meeting-house. The feeling of coöperation so noticeable in all men and growing communities, and which is really essential for their success, is aptly described in the old "Annals of Tennessee," published by Dr. J. G. M. Ramsey in 1853 ("Dedicated to the surviving pioneers of Tennessee"): [1]

"To say of one he has no neighbours was sufficient, in those times of mutual wants and mutual benefactions, to make the churl infamous and execrable. A failure to ask a neighbour to a raising, clearing, a chopping frolic, or his family to a quilting, was considered a high indignity; such an one, too, as required to be explained or atoned for at the next muster or county court. Each settler was not only willing but desirous to contribute his share to the general comfort and public improvement, and felt aggrieved and insulted if the opportunity to do so were withheld. 'It is a poor dog that is not worth whistling for,' replied the indignant neighbour who was allowed to remain at home, at his own work, while a house raising was going on in the neighbourhood. 'What injury have I done that I am slighted so?'"

Quilts occupied a preëminent place in the rural social scheme, and the quilting bees were one of the few social diversions afforded outside of the church. Much drudgery was lightened by the joyful anticipation of a neighbourhood quilting bee. The preparations for such an important event were often quite elaborate. As a form of entertainment quilting bees have stood the test of time, and from colonial days down to the present have furnished much pleasure in country communities.

In a quaint little book published in 1872 by Mrs. P. G. Gibbons, under the title, "Pennsylvania Dutch," is a detailed description of a country quilting that Mrs. Gibbons attended. The exact date of this social affair is not given, but judging from other closely related incidents mentioned by the writer, it must have taken place about 1840, in Lancaster County, Pennsylvania. The account reads as follows: [2]

"Aunt Sally had her quilt up in her landlord's east room, for her own was too small. However, at about eleven she called us over to dinner, for people who have breakfasted at five or six have an appetite at eleven.

"We found on the table beefsteaks, boiled pork, sweet potatoes, 'Kohl-slaw,' pickled cucumbers and red beets, apple butter and preserved peaches, pumpkin and apple pie, sponge cake and coffee. After dinner came our next neighbours, 'the maids,' Susy and Katy Groff, who live in single blessedness and great neatness. They wore pretty, clear-starched Mennonist caps, very plain. Katy is a sweet-looking woman and, although she is more than

VIRGINIA ROSE

This original rose design was made by Caroline Stalnaker of Lewis County, West Virginia. She was one of the thirteen children of Charles Stalnaker, who was a "rock-ribbed" Baptist, and an ardent Northern sympathizer. During the Civil War this quilt was buried along with the family silver and other valuables to protect it from depredations by Confederate soldiers. One of Caroline Stalnaker's neighbors and friends was Stonewall Jackson.

In this quilt, as in many old ones, the border has been omitted on the side intended to go at the head of the bed. This quilt is still unfinished, having never been quilted.

FIGURE 53

ROSE OF LEMOINE

An old and distinctly American design

FIGURE 54

sixty years old, her forehead is almost unwrinkled, and her fine hair is still brown. It was late when the farmer's wife came—three o'clock; for she had been to Lancaster. She wore hoops and was of the 'world's people.' These women all spoke 'Dutch,' for the maids, whose ancestors came here probably one hundred and fifty years ago, do not speak English with fluency yet.

"The first subject of conversation was the fall house-cleaning; and I heard mention of 'die carpett hinaus an der fence' and 'die fenshter und die porch,' and the exclamation, 'My goodness, es was schlimm.' I quilted faster than Katy Groff, who showed me her hands, and said, 'You have not been corn husking, as I have.'

"So we quilted and rolled, talked and laughed, got one quilt done, and put in another. The work was not fine; we laid it out by chalking around a small plate. Aunt Sally's desire was rather to get her quilting finished upon this great occasion than for us to put in a quantity of fine needlework. About five o'clock we were called to supper. I need not tell you all the particulars of this plentiful meal; but the stewed chicken was tender and we had coffee again.

"Polly M's husband now came over the creek in the boat, to take her home, and he warned her against the evening dampness. The rest of us quilted a while by candles, and got the second quilt done at about seven. At this quilting there was little gossip, and less scandal. I displayed my new alpaca and my dyed merino and the Philadelphia bonnet which exposes the back of my head to the wintry blast. Polly, for her part, preferred a black silk sunbonnet; and so we parted, with mutual invitations to visit."

The proverbial neatness of the ancestors of the Dutch colonists in America was characteristic of their homes in the new land. This is well illustrated in the following description of a Pennsylvania Dutch farmer's home, similar to the one in which the quilting above mentioned took place:[3] "We keep one fire in winter. This is in the kitchen which, with nice housekeepers, is the abode of neatness, with its rag carpet and brightly polished stove. Adjoining the kitchen is a state apartment, also rag-carpeted, and called 'the room.' Will you go upstairs in a neat Dutch farmhouse? There are rag carpets again. Gay quilts are on the best beds, where green and red calico, perhaps in the

CHARTER OAK

With the American eagle in the border

FIGURE 55

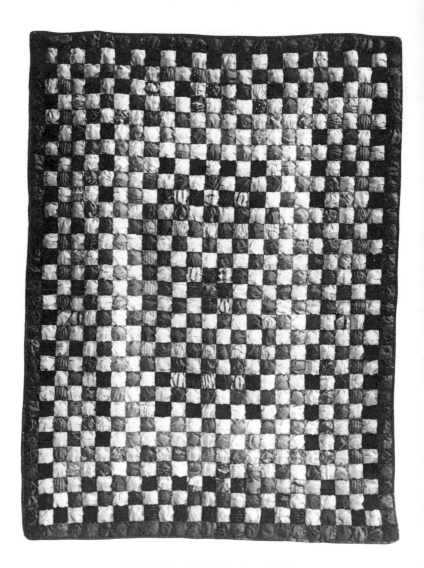

PUFFED QUILT OF SILK

This is a very popular pieced quilt, composed of carefully saved bits of silks and velvets.

FIGURE 56

form of a basket, are displayed on a white ground; or the beds bear brilliant coverlets of red, white, and blue, as if to 'make the rash gazer wipe his eyes.'"

There are many things to induce women to piece quilts. The desire for a handsome bed furnishing, or the wish to make a gift of one to a dear friend, have inspired some women to make quilts. With others, quilt making is a recreation, a diversion, a means of occupying restless fingers. However, the real inducement is love of the work; because the desire to make a quilt exceeds all other desires. In such a case it is worked on persistently, laid aside reluctantly, and taken up each time with renewed interest and pleasure. It is this intense interest in the work which produces the most beautiful quilts. On quilts that are made because of the genuine interest in the work, the most painstaking efforts are put forth; the passing of time is not considered; and the belief of the majority of such quilt makers, though unconfessed, doubtless, is the equivalent of the old Arab proverb that "Slowness comes from God, but hurry from the devil."

All women who are lonely do not live in isolated farmhouses, prairie shacks, or remote villages. In reality, there are more idle, listless hands in the hearts of crowded bustling cities than in the quiet country. City women, surrounded by many enticing distractions, are turning more and more to patchwork as a fascinating yet nerve-soothing occupation. Not only is there a sort of companionship between the maker and the quilt, but there is also the great benefit derived from having found a new interest in life, something worth while that can be built up by one's own efforts.

An anecdote is told of a woman living in a quiet little New England village who complained of her loneliness there, where the quilting bees were the only saving features of an otherwise colourless existence. She told the interested listener that in this out-of-the-way hamlet she did not mind the monotony much because there were plenty of "quiltings," adding that she had helped that winter at more than twenty-five quilting bees; besides this, she had made a quilt for herself and also helped on some of those of her immediate neighbours.

American women rarely think of quilts as being made or used outside of their own country. In reality quilts are made in almost every land on the

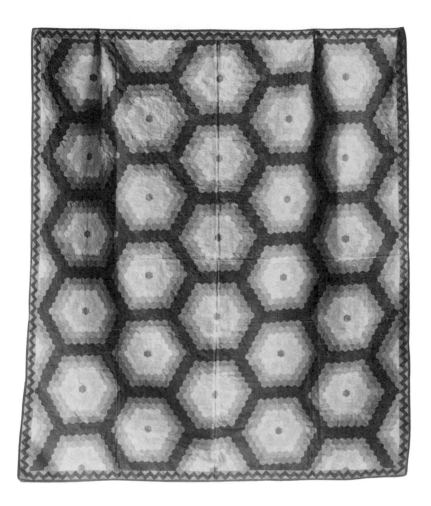

VARIEGATED HEXAGON, SILK
Colours: cherry, light blue, pink, black, and a yellow
centre

FIGURE 57

ROMAN STRIPE, SILK

FIGURE 58

face of the earth. Years ago, when the first New England missionaries were sent to the Hawaiian Islands, the native women were taught to piece quilts, which they continue to do down to this day. These Hawaiian women treasure their handiwork greatly, and some very old and beautiful quilts are to be found among these islands. In creating their patchwork they have wandered from the Puritanical designs of their teachers, and have intermingled with the conventional figures the gorgeous flowers that bloom beside their leaf-thatched, vine-covered huts. To these women, also, patchwork fills a place. It affords a means of expression for individuality and originality in the same way that it does for the lonely New England women and for the isolated mountaineers of Kentucky. [4]

Harriet Beecher Stowe, immortalized by "Uncle Tom's Cabin," produced other stories, not now so familiar to us as to our countrymen of the Civil War period, which showed an intimate knowledge of the home life of the American people as well as the vital questions of her day. In her novel entitled the "Minister's Wooing," which ran first as a serial in the *Atlantic Monthly* in 1859, she describes a quilting supposed to have been given about the year 1800. Here we can view at close range a real old-fashioned quilting, and gain some insight into its various incidents of sociability and gossip, typical of an early New England seafaring village, as set forth in Mrs. Stowe's inimitable style: [5]

"By two o'clock a goodly company began to assemble. Mrs. Deacon Twitchel arrived, soft, pillowy, and plaintive as ever, accompanied by Cerinthy Ann, a comely damsel, tall and trim, with a bright black eye and a most vigorous and determined style of movement. Good Mrs. Jones, broad, expansive, and solid, having vegetated tranquilly on in the cabbage garden of the virtues since three years ago, when she graced our tea party, was now as well preserved as ever, and brought some fresh butter, a tin pail of cream, and a loaf of cake made after a new Philadelphia receipt. The tall, spare, angular figure of Mrs. Simeon Brown alone was wanting; but she patronized Mrs. Scudder no more, and tossed her head with a becoming pride when her name was mentioned.

"The quilt pattern was gloriously drawn in oak leaves, done in indigo; and soon all the company, young and old, were passing busy fingers over it, and conversation went on briskly.

"Madame de Frontignac, we must not forget to say, had entered with hearty abandon into the spirit of the day. She had dressed the tall china vases on the mantelpiece, and, departing from the usual rule of an equal mixture of roses and asparagus bushes, had constructed two quaint and graceful bouquets where garden flowers were mingled with drooping grasses and trailing wild vines, forming a graceful combination which excited the surprise of all who saw it.

"'It's the very first time in my life that I ever saw grass put into a flower pot,' said Miss Prissy, 'but I must say it looks as handsome as a picture. Mary, I must say,' she added, in an aside, 'I think that Madame de Frontignac is the sweetest dressing and appearing creature I ever saw; she don't dress up nor put on airs, but she seems to see in a minute how things ought to go; and if it's only a bit of grass, or leaf, or wild vine, that she puts in her hair, why, it seems to come just right. I should like to make her a dress, for I know she would understand my fit; do speak to her, Mary, in case she should want a dress fitted here, to let me try it.'

"At the quilting Madame de Frontignac would have her seat, and soon won the respect of the party by the dexterity with which she used her needle; though, when it was whispered that she learned to quilt among the nuns, some of the elderly ladies exhibited a slight uneasiness, as being rather doubtful whether they might not be encouraging papistical opinions by allowing her an equal share in the work of getting up their minister's bed quilt; but the younger part of the company was quite captivated by her foreign air and the pretty manner in which she lisped her English; and Cerinthy Ann even went so far as to horrify her mother by saying that she wished she'd been educated in a convent herself, a declaration which arose less from native depravity than from a certain vigorous disposition, which often shows itself in young people, to shock the current opinions of their elders and betters. Of course, the conversation took a general turn, somewhat in unison with the spirit of the occasion; and whenever it flagged, some allusion to a forthcoming wedding, or some sly hint at the future young Madame of the parish was sufficient to awaken the dormant animation of the company.

AMERICAN LOG CABIN, SILK AND WOOL
In Colonial days this was known as a "pressed" quilt.

FIGURE 59

DEMOCRAT ROSE
Made in Pennsylvania about 1845.

FIGURE 60

"Cerinthy Ann contrived to produce an agreeable electric shock by declaring that for her part she never could see into it how any girl could marry a minister; that she should as soon think of setting up housekeeping in a meeting-house.

"'Oh, Cerinthy Ann!' exclaimed her mother, 'how can you go on so?'

"'It's a fact,' said the adventurous damsel; 'now other men let you have some peace, but a minister's always round under your feet.'

"'So you think the less you see of a husband, the better?' said one of the ladies.

"'Just my views!' said Cerinthy, giving a decided snip to her thread with her scissors. 'I like the Nantucketers, that go off on four years' voyages, and leave their wives a clear field. If ever I get married, I'm going up to have one of those fellows.'

"It is to be remarked, in passing, that Miss Cerinthy Ann was at this very time receiving surreptitious visits from a consumptive-looking, conscientious young theological candidate, who came occasionally to preach in the vicinity, and put up at the house of the deacon, her father. This good young man, being violently attacked on the doctrine of election by Miss Cerinthy, had been drawn on to illustrate it in a most practical manner, to her comprehension; and it was the consciousness of the weak and tottering state of the internal garrison that added vigour to the young lady's tones. As Mary had been the chosen confidante of the progress of this affair, she was quietly amused at the demonstration.

" 'You'd better take care, Cerinthy Ann,' said her mother, 'they say " that those who sing before breakfast will cry before supper." Girls talk about getting married,' she said, relapsing into a gentle melancholy, 'without realizing its awful responsibilities.'

" 'Oh, as to that,' said Cerinthy, 'I've been practising on my pudding now these six years, and I shouldn't be afraid to throw one up chimney with any girl.'

"This speech was founded on a tradition, current in those times, that no young lady was fit to be married till she could construct a boiled Indian pudding of such consistency that it could be thrown up a chimney and come down on the ground outside without breaking; and the consequence of Cerinthy Ann's sally was a general laugh.

"'Girls ain't what they used to be in my day,' sententiously remarked an elderly lady. 'I remember my mother told me when she was thirteen she could knit a long cotton stocking in a day.'

"'I haven't much faith in these stories of old times, have you, girls?' said Cerinthy, appealing to the younger members at the frame.

"'At any rate,' said Mrs. Twitchel, 'our minister's wife will be a pattern; I don't know anybody that goes beyond her either in spinning or fine stitching.'

"Mary sat as placid and disengaged as the new moon, and listened to the chatter of old and young with the easy quietness of a young heart that has early outlived life and looks on everything in the world from some gentle, restful eminence far on toward a better home. She smiled at everybody's word, had a quick eye for everybody's wants, and was ready with thimble, scissors, or thread, whenever any one needed them; but once, when there was a pause in the conversation, she and Mrs. Marvyn were both discovered to have stolen away. They were seated on the bed in Mary's little room, with their arms around each other, communing in low and gentle tones.

"'Mary, my dear child,' said her friend, 'this event is very pleasant to me, because it places you permanently near me. I did not know but eventually this sweet face might lead to my losing you who are in some respects the dearest friend I have.'

"'You might be sure,' said Mary, 'I never would have married, except that my mother's happiness and the happiness of so good a friend seemed to depend on it. When we renounce self in anything we have reason to hope for God's blessing; and so I feel assured of a peaceful life in the course I have taken. You will always be as a mother to me,' she added, laying her head on her friend's shoulder.

"'Yes,' said Mrs. Marvyn; 'and I must not let myself think a moment how dear it might have been to have you more my own. If you feel really, truly happy, if you can enter on this life without any misgivings——'

"'I can,' said Mary firmly.

"At this instant, very strangely, the string which confined a wreath of seashells around her glass, having been long undermined by moths, suddenly broke and fell down, scattering the shells upon the floor.

ORIGINAL ROSE NO. 3
Made in Indiana about 75 years ago.   Colors: red and green.

FIGURE 61

WHITE QUILT, WITH STUFFED QUILTING DESIGNS

This quilt was made in New England, and was finished in 1801, but how long a period was occupied in the making is unknown. It was designed by a young architect for an ambitious young quilter

FIGURE 62

"Both women started, for the string of shells had been placed there by James; and though neither was superstitious, this was one of those odd coincidences that make hearts throb.

"'Dear boy!' said Mary, gathering the shells up tenderly; 'wherever he is, I shall never cease to love him. It makes me feel sad to see this come down; but it is only an accident; nothing of him will ever fall out of my heart.'

"Mrs. Marvyn clasped Mary closer to her, with tears in her eyes.

"'I'll tell you what, Mary, it must have been the moths did that,' said Miss Prissy, who had been standing, unobserved, at the door for a moment back; 'moths will eat away strings just so. Last week Miss Vernon's great family picture fell down because the moths eat through the cord; people ought to use twine or cotton string always. But I came to tell you that supper is all set, and the doctor out of his study, and all the people are wondering where you are.'

"Mary and Mrs. Marvyn gave a hasty glance at themselves in the glass, to be assured of their good keeping, and went into the great kitchen, where a long table stood exhibiting all that plentitude of

[165]

provision which the immortal description of Washington Irving has saved us the trouble of recapitulating in detail.

"The husbands, brothers, and lovers had come in, and the scene was redolent of gayety. When Mary made her appearance, there was a moment's pause, till she was conducted to the side of the doctor; when, raising his hand, he invoked a grace upon the loaded board.

"Unrestrained gayeties followed. Groups of young men and maidens chatted together, and all the gallantries of the times were enacted. Serious matrons commented on the cake, and told each other high and particular secrets in the culinary art which they drew from remote family archives. One might have learned in that instructive assembly how best to keep moths out of blankets, how to make fritters of Indian corn undistinguishable from oysters, how to bring up babies by hand, how to mend a cracked teapot, how to take out grease from a brocade, how to reconcile absolute decrees with free will, how to make five yards of cloth answer the purpose of six, and how to put down the Democratic party.

"Miss Prissy was in her glory; every bow of her

best cap was alive with excitement, and she presented to the eyes of the astonished Newport gentry an animated receipt book. Some of the information she communicated, indeed, was so valuable and important that she could not trust the air with it, but whispered the most important portions in a confidential tone. Among the crowd, Cerinthy Ann's theological admirer was observed in deeply reflective attitude; and that high-spirited young lady added further to his convictions of the total depravity of the species by vexing and discomposing him in those thousand ways in which a lively, ill-conditioned young woman will put to rout a serious, well-disposed young man, comforting herself with the reflection that by and by she would repent of all her sins in a lump together.

"Vain, transitory splendours! Even this evening, so glorious, so heart cheering, so fruitful in instruction and amusement, could not last forever. Gradually the company broke up; the matrons mounted soberly on horseback behind their spouses, and Cerinthy consoled her clerical friend by giving him an opportunity to read her a lecture on the way home, if he found the courage to do so.

"Mr. and Mrs. Marvyn and Candace wound their

way soberly homeward; the doctor returned to his study for nightly devotions; and before long sleep settled down on the brown cottage.

"'I'll tell you what, Cato,' said Candace, before composing herself to sleep, 'I can't feel it in my bones dat dis yer weddin's gwine to come off yit.'"

WHITE QUILT

A very beautiful and original design, made in New England over 125 years ago. Only part of the design has been stuffed

FIGURE 63

QUILTS ON A LINE

FIGURE 64

LIST OF QUILT NAMES

ARRANGED ALPHABETICALLY

Air Castle
Alabama Beauty
Album
All Tangled Up
Alpine Rose
American Log Patch
Apple Hexagon
Arabic Lattice
Arkansas Traveller
Art Square
Ashland Rose
Aunt Eliza's Star Quilt
Aunt Sukey's Patch
Autograph Quilt

Bachelor's Puzzle
Barrister's Blocks
Baseball
Basket of Lilies
Basket Quilt
Bat's Wing
Bear's Foot
Bear's Paws
Bedtime

Beggar's Blocks
Big Dipper
Bird's Nest
Blackford's Beauty
Blazing Star
Blindman's Fancy
Block Album
Bluebird
Boston Puzzle
Bounding Betty
Bouquet
Box Blocks
Boxed I's
Boy's Nonsense
Brick Pile
Brickwork Quilt
Broken Dish
Brown-tailed Moth
Brunswick Star
Bunnies
Bunnies and Baskets
Butterflies
Cactus Blossom
Cake Stand

California Oak Leaf
California Rose
California Star
Capital I
Carolina Lily
Carpenter's Rule
Carpenter's Square
Cats and Mice
Centennial
Charm
Charter Oak
Cherry Basket
Chicago Star
Children's Delight
Chimney Swallows
Christmas Tree
Chrysanthemums
Churn Dash
Circle Within Circle
Circuit Rider
Cleveland Lilies
Cluster of Stars
Coarse Woven Patch
Cockscomb
Cogwheels
Columbian Puzzle
Columbia Star
Combination Star
Compass
Complex Rose
Confederate Rose
Continental
Corn and Beans

Cottage Tulip
Country Farm
Coxey's Camp
Crazy Ann
Crazy Quilt
Crib Quilt
Cross, The
Cross and Crown
Crosses and Losses
Crosses and Stars
Crossed Canoes
Cross Roads to Texas
Cross Within Cross
Crow's Foot
Cube Lattice
Cube Work
Cypress Leaf

Daffodils and Butterflies
Daisies
Democrat Rose
Devil's Claws
Devil's Puzzle
Diagonal Log Chain
Diamond, The
Diamond Cube
Diamond Design
Diamonds
Diamond Star
Disk, The
Dogwood
Domino
Domino and Square

Double Irish Chain
Double Peony
Double Square
Double Wrench
Double X, No. 1
Double X, No. 2
Double X, No. 3
Double X, No. 4
Double Z
Dove in the Window
Dutchman's Puzzle
Dutch Rose
Drunkard's Patchwork
Drunkard's Path
Duck and Ducklings

Ecclesiastical
Economy
Eight Hands Around
Eight-point Design
Eight-pointed Star
Enigma
Evening Star
Everybody's Favourite

Fan
Fan and Rainbow
Fan Patch
Fanny's Fan
Fantastic Patch
Feather Star
Ferris Wheel
Field Daisies

Five-pointed Star
Five Stripes
Fleur de Lis
Flower Basket
Flower Pot
Flutter Wheel
Flying Bat
Flying Star
Fool's Puzzle
Fool's Square
Forbidden Fruit Tree
Forest Pattern
Four E's
Four Frog's Quilt
Four Little Birds
Four Points
Four Star's Patch
Four X Star
French Baskets
Friendship Quilt
Fruit Basket

Garden of Eden
Garfield's Monument
Gentleman's Fancy
Georgetown Circle
Girl's Joy
Globe, The
Golden Gates
Goose in the Pond
Goose Tracks
Gourd Vine
Grandmother's Choice

Grandmother's Dream
Grandmother's Own
Grape Basket
Grapes and Vines
Grecian Design
Greek Cross
Greek Square

Hair Pin Catcher
Hand, The
Hands All Around
Handy Andy
Harrison Rose
Harvest Rose
Hearts and Gizzards
Hen and Chickens
Hexagonal
Hickory Leaf
Hobson's Kiss
Home Treasure
Honeycomb
Honeycomb Patch
Hour Glass
House That Jack Built

Ice Cream Bowl
Imperial Tea
Indiana Wreath
Indian Hatchet
Indian Plums
Interlaced Blocks
Iris
Irish Puzzle

Jack's House
Jacob's Ladder
Job's Tears
Johnny Around the Corner
Joining Star
Jonquils
Joseph's Coat
Joseph's Necktie

Kansas Troubles
King's Crown
King's Crows

Ladies' Beautiful Star
Ladies' Delight
Ladies' Wreath
Lady Fingers
Lady of the Lake
Leap Frog
Letter H
Letter X
Lily of the Valley
Lily Quilt Pattern
Lincoln's Platform
Linton
Little Beech Tree
Little Red House, The
Live Oak Tree
Lobster, The
Log Cabin
Log Patch
London Roads
Love Rose

[172]

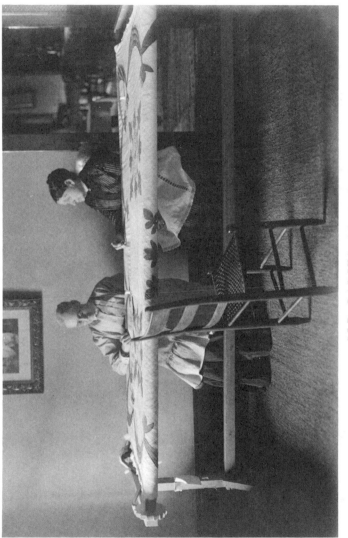

OLD LADIES QUILTING

FIGURE 65

GRAPES AND VINES

FIGURE 66

Lover's Links
Magic Circle
Maltese Cross, No. 1
Maltese Cross, No. 2
Maple Leaf
Mary's Garden
May Berry Leaf
Mayflower, The
Memory Blocks
Memory Circle
Mexican Rose
Missouri Beauty
Mollie's Choice
Moon and Stars
Morning Glory
Morning Glory Wreath
Morning Star
Mosaic (More than 25)
Mother's Fancy
Mrs. Cleveland's Choice
Mrs. Morgan's Choice

Needlebook
Necktie
New Album
New Four Patch
Nine Patch
New Star
No Name Quilt
None Such
Novel Star
Oak Leaf and Acorns
Oak Leaf and Tulip

Ocean Waves
Octagon
Octagon File
Odd Fellows' Chain
Odd Patchwork
Odd Pattern, An
Odds and Ends
Odd Star
Ohio Beauty
Oklahoma Boomer
Old Homestead, The
Old Maid's Puzzle
Old Patchwork, An
Old Scrap Patchwork
Old Bachelor's Puzzle
Old Tippecanoe
Olive Branch
Orange Peel

Paving Blocks
Pansies and Butterflies
Peacocks and Flowers
Peony Block
Persian Palm Lily
Philadelphia Beauty
Philadelphia Pavement
Philippines, The
Pickle Dish
Pilgrim's Pride
Pincushion
Pincushion and Burr
Pineapple Patterns (3 in number)

[173]

Pine Tree
Pinwheel Square
Poinsettia
Poppy
Prairie Rose
Premium Star
President's Quilt
Princess Feather
Priscilla, The
Pullman Puzzle
Puss-in-the-Corner
Puzzle File
Pyrotechnics

Quartette, The

Radical Rose
Railroad, The
Rainbow
Red Cross
Ribbon Squares
Ribbon Star
Right and Left
Rising Sun
Road to Oklahoma
Robbing Peter to Pay Paul
Rockingham's Beauty
Rocky Glen
Rocky Road to California
Rocky Road to Kansas
Rolling Pinwheel
Rolling Star
Rolling Stone

Roman Cross
Roman Stripe
Rose
Rose Album
Rose and Feather
Rosebud and Leaves
Rose of Dixie
Rose of Le Moine
Rose of St. Louis
Rose of the Carolinas
Rose of Sharon
Rose Sprig
Royal, The
Royal Japanese Vase

St. Louis Star
Sarah's Favourite
Sashed Album
Sashed Star
Sawtooth Patchwork
Scissors' Chain
Seven Stars
Shelf Chain
Shield
Shoo Fly
Shooting Star
Simple Design
Single Sunflowers
Sister's Choice
Snail's Trail, The
Snowball
Snowflake
Solomon's Temple

[174]

Solomon's Crown
Spider's Den
Spider's Web
Spools
Square and a Half
Square and Swallow
Square and Triangle
Square Log Cabin
Squares and Stars
Squares and Stripes
Star, A
Star and Chains
Star and Cross
Star and Cubes
Star and Squares
Star of Bethlehem
Star of Many Points
Star of Texas
Star of the East
Star Lane
Star Puzzle
Star-Spangled Banner
Stars upon Stars
State House Steps
Steps to the Altar
St. Louis Star
Stone Wall
Storm at Sea
Strawberry
Stripe Squares
Sugar Loaf
Sunbonnet Lassies
Sunburst

Sunflowers
Sunshine
Swarm of Bees
Sweet Gum Leaf
Swinging Corners
Swing in the Centre

Tangled Garter
Tassel Plant
Tea Leaf
Temperance Tree
Texas Flower
Texas Tears
Three-flowered Sunflower
Tick-Tack-Toe
Tile Patchwork
Toad in the Puddle
Tree of Paradise
Triangular Triangle
Triangle Puzzle
True Lover's Knot
Tufted Cherry
Tulip Blocks
Tulip in Vase
Tulip Lady Finger
Tulip Tree Leaves
Tumbler, The
Twin Sisters
Twinkling Star
Twist and Turn
Twist Patchwork
Two Doves, The

Union

Union Calico Quilt

Union Star

Unknown Star

Valentine Quilt

Variegated Diamonds

Variegated Hexagons

Venetian Design

Vestibule

Vice-President's Quilt

Village Church

Virginia Gentleman

Washington Puzzle

Washington's Plumes

Washington's Sidewalk

Watered Ribbon

Way of the World

Wedding Knot

Western Star

W. C. T. Union

Wheel, The

Wheel and Star

Wheel of Fortune

Whig Pattern

Whig Rose

White Day Lily

Widower's Choice

Wild Goose Chase

Wild Rose

Wind-blown Tulips

Winding Walk

Windmill

Wonder of the World

Workbox

World's Fair, The

World's Fair Blocks

World's Fair Puzzle

Wreath of Roses

Xquisite, The

Yankee Puzzle

Beautifully made old quilt. Designs cut from chintz are appliqued to white blocks; the quilting designs on the plain blocks repeat the coloured design in outline. This quilt was taken from a Southern home by a soldier who was with Sherman on his famous "march to the sea." Owned in Madison, Wisconsin.

FIGURE 67

Interesting old quilt made about 1800. Foundation faded pale green.
Made in Canada. Owned in Madison, Wisconsin.

FIGURE 68

LIST OF REFERENCES

THE CAROLINA MOUNTAINA. *Margaret M. Morley.*

THE MINISTER'S WOOING. *Harriet Beecher Stowe.*

AUNT JANE IN KENTUCKY. *Hall.*

COLONIAL DAYS AND WAYS. *Helen Evesten Smith.*

THE STORY OF THE CITY OF NEW YORK. *Charles Burr Todd,* 1888.

THE SOCIAL HISTORY OF FLATBUSH. *Gertrude Lefferts Vanderbilt,* 1882.

SOCIAL HISTORY OF ANCIENT IRELAND. *P. W. Joyce.*

CHATS ON OLD LACE AND NEEDLEWORK. *Mrs. Lowes.*

THE CRUSADES. *Archer and Kingsford.*

THE LURE OF THE ANTIQUE. *Walter A. Dyer.*

ART AND NEEDLEWORK. *Lewis M. Day and Mary Buckle.*

HOME LIFE IN COLONIAL DAYS. *Alice Morse Earle.*

CUSTOMS AND FASHIONS IN OLD NEW ENGLAND. *Alice Morse Earle.*

PENNSYLVANIA DUTCH. *Mrs. P. E. Gibbon.*

ON EDUCATION. *John Locke,* 1632-1704.

OLD EMBROIDERIES. *Alam S. Cole in Home Needlework Magazine,* 1900-1901.

THE ANNALS OF TENNESSEE. *J. G. M. Ramsey, A. M., M. D.,* 1853.

WOMAN'S HANDIWORK IN MODERN HOMES. *Constance Cary Harrison,* 1881.

PEASANT ART IN SWEDEN, IRELAND, AND LAPLAND. *Edited by Charles Holmes.*

FIRST STEPS IN COLLECTING. *Grace M. Vallois.*

LIST OF REFERENCES

NEEDLEWORK. *Elizabeth Glaister.*

EMBROIDERY AND TAPESTRY WEAVING. *Mrs. A. H. Christie.*

THE ART OF NEEDLEWORK. *Edited by Countess Wilton.*

ENGLISH SECULAR EMBROIDERY. *M. Jourdain.*

THE ANCIENT EGYPTIANS. *Sir. J. Gardner Wilkinson, S. C. L., F. R. S.*

DE BELLO JUDAICS. *Flavius Josephus.*

TURKEY OF THE OTTOMAN. *L. M. Garnett.*

HISTOIRE DE L'ART DAMS L'ANTIQUITÉ. *Perrot and Chipiez.*

ARTS AND CRAFTS IN THE MIDDLE AGES. *Julia de Wolf Addison.*

SACO VALLEY FAMILIES. *Ridlon.*

Beautifully made dark blue and white quilt. Owned in Madison, Wisconsin.

FIGURE 69

This quilt was made by a native of Hawaii. The design shows strongly the influence of the luxuriant vegetation found in the Hawaiian Islands. It was named by the maker, "Rain Falling in Honolulu."

FIGURE 70

NOTES

Chapter I

1. Naamah is mentioned in Genesis 4:22. The Phrygians, possibly of Thracian descent, dominated Asia Minor from the 12th to the 7th centuries B.C. They excelled in metalwork and wood carving and are said to have invented the art of embroidery.

   Huang-ti, "The Yellow Emperor," and his wife Si-Ling-Chi are regarded as legendary rather than strictly historical figures. He is credited with regulating the calendar and building the first cities. Besides inventing the loom, Si-Ling-Chi is said to have discovered the secret of obtaining strands of thread from the cocoons of silkworms. (Ethel Lewis, *The Romance of Textiles*, New York: Macmillan, 1937, pp. 31–32.)

2. Sir John Gardner Wilkinson, *A Popular Account of the Ancient Egyptians* (New York: Harper & Brothers, 1854), Vol. 2, pp. 72–73, 83.

3. Wilkinson (Vol. 2, p. 81) cites several Biblical verses from Exodus, 26:36; 27:16; 28:39; 36:37; 38:18; 39:3 and 39:29.

   Flavius Josephus was the Roman name taken by the Jewish priest and scholar Joseph Ben Matthias (ca. 37– ca. 100 A.D.). His famous history, *De Bello Judaico*, described the siege of Jerusalem in 75–79 A.D. from a pro-Roman point of view. One recent edition is *The Jewish War*, translated by G.A. Williamson (Harmondsworth: Penguin Books, 1970), where this description of the temple tapestry appears on p. 293.

4. The Egyptian hanging of the boy and goose is described in Wilkinson (Vol. 2, p. 92) as a small rug, 9 x 11 inches, "made like many carpets of the present day, with woollen threads on linen string." The Biblical reference is to Psalm 45:13–14.

5. Wilkinson, Vol. 2, pp. 322–323.

6. Alan S. Cole, "Old Embroideries," Part 1, *Home Needlework Magazine*, July 1900, pp. 178–179. See Fig. 1 for an illustration of the tent taken from p. 174 of Cole's article. Discovered in 1875 in the Deir el-Bahari cache at Thebes, the tent was made to cover the coffin of Queen Isimkhabiu during her funeral ceremony. The surviving fragments are in the collection of the Egyptian Museum in Cairo; a photograph appears in *The History of the Patchwork Quilt*, by Schnuppe von Gwinner (West Chester, PA: Schiffer Publishing, 1988), p. 20, Fig. 8.

7. The story of Arachne is told by the Roman poet Ovid in his *Metamorphoses* (Book VI, 5–145). Pallas Athene, warrior daughter of Zeus and goddess of wisdom, was worshipped in Athens as the patron of domestic arts, especially spinning and weaving.

8. Penelope's ruse is recounted in Book II of Homer's *Odyssey.*

Chapter II

1. In the fifth century A.D., Bishop Asterius of Pontus is said to have preached against the excessively ornamented clothing of the wealthy, "who wore the Gospels on their backs instead of in their hearts." Quoted in Alan S. Cole, "Old Embroideries," Part 1, *Home Needlework Magazine*, July 1900, p. 182.

2. This beautiful example of medieval embroidery, thought to date from about 1320, is illustrated in Figure 5 and further discussed in Chapter III, p. 35. Stonyhurst College is a famous Jesuit school in northern England.

3. This quilt is described and illustrated in Margaret S. Burton, "Old Bed-spreads, Quilts, and Coverlets — An Alluring Field for the Collector," *Country Life in America,* 15 Dec. 1910, pp. 197–198. Stanford White (1853–1906) was a prominent New York architect whose achievements have been overshadowed by the scandal of his murder. He was shot to death by the jealous husband of his mistress, showgirl Evelyn Nesbit, in the old Madison Square Garden, a building of his own design.

4. In his *Lives of the Italian Painters, Sculptors and Architects* (1568), Giorgio Vasari remarks that "It was by Sandro Botticelli that the method of preparing banners and standards in what is called cut-work was invented; and this he did that the colours might not sink through, showing the tint of the cloth on each side."

Julia de Wolf Addison in *Arts and Crafts in the Middle Ages* (London: G. Bell, 1908), pp. 190–191, states that Botticelli employed two kinds of appliqué: one in which linen was embroidered with silks before being applied to a brocade background, and the other, a simple appliqué with the raw edges concealed by a cord. "As an improvement upon painted banners to be used in processions, Botticelli introduced this method of cutting out and resetting colours upon a different ground." Addison adds a note of caution: "it is hardly fair to earlier artificers to give the entire credit for this method of work to Botticelli, since such cut work or appliqué was practised in Italy a hundred years before Botticelli was born!"

5.   Although the term *opus consutum*, or "cut work," usually refers to the technique of appliqué, it can also refer to Madeira work or *broderie anglaise*, in which holes are pierced in linen and then overcast. See Grace Christie, *Embroidery and Tapestry Weaving* (London: J. Hogg, 1915), pp. 221–228.

6.   Daniel Rock, *Textile Fabrics* (South Kensington Museum Art Handbook No. 1; New York: Scribner, Welford & Armstrong, 1876), pp. 88–89.

7.   The South Kensington Museum was renamed the Victoria and Albert Museum in 1899. Now Britain's National Museum of Art and Design, it contains a world famous collection of decorative arts, including many superb textiles.

8.   A gimp is a flat trimming of cord, sometimes stiffened with wire.

9.   Christie, pp. 180–183; also Lewis F. Day and Mary Buckle, *Art in Needlework* (London: B. T. Batsford, 1900), pp. 153–156.

10. A. F. Kendrick, in his introduction to *A Book of Old Embroidery* (edited by Geoffrey Holme; London: The Studio, 1921), pp. 13–14 and Plate 39, calls this quilt "one of the most valuable existing essays in mediaeval story-telling by embroidery." The entire piece was originally over 15 feet square and consisted of 16 panels and a wide border, with inscriptions in Sicilian. Part of the quilt is in the Victoria and Albert Museum in London and the rest, known as the "Coperta Guicciardini," is in the Museo Nazionale in Florence, Italy. (Marie Schuette and Sigrid Müller-Christensen, *A Pictorial History of Embroidery,* New York: Frederick A. Praeger, 1964, Plate 169.) Webster's source was Christie, *Embroidery and Tapestry Weaving,* pp. 357–358 and Plate III, which shows a detail: "How King Languis (of Ireland) sent to Cornwall for the tribute." ("Langair" is a typographical error.) The quilt was later discussed and illustrated by Carrie A. Hall and Rose G. Kretsinger in *The Romance of the Patchwork Quilt in America* (1935; reprint ed., New York: Bonanza Books), pp. 264, 266, 288–289.

11. See Fig. 7 for a picture of the Persian quilted bath or prayer carpet. The source for both the description and illustration was Alan S. Cole, "Old Embroideries," Part 3, *Home Needlework Magazine,* January 1901, pp. 8–11.

12. Lucy M. Garnett, *Turkey of the Ottomans* (New York: Scribner's, 1911), p. 279. There are three typographical errors in this paragraph: the first in the name of the hero, which should be "Nasr-ed-Din Hodja"; the second demotes him from the rank of a "Turkish parson" to the common status of a "Turkish person"; the third omits the final "s" from the title of the book. On p. 179, Garnett explains that a *hodja* is the village priest who climbs the minaret of the mosque five times a day to call the faithful to prayer; this term is presumably related to *hadji,* a title of honor for any Moslem who has completed his pilgrimage to Mecca.

13. This piece is illustrated in Margaret Jourdain, *English Secular Embroidery* (New York: E.P. Dutton, 1912), facing p. 20 and described on pp. 19–20: "It certainly reflects the style of drawing and composition of illuminated manuscripts of the fourteenth century.... Under triple canopies are primitively drawn groups of kings, horses, and dragons, cut out of coloured cloths patched together and applied. The ornament is outlined by strips of blackened vellum (formerly gilt) stitched down. The border at the top consists of groups of knights and ladies conversing, each within a separate arch."

14. This paragraph is based on sections from the chapter amusingly entitled "The Flotsam and Jetsam of Old Lumber Rooms" in Grace M. Vallois, *First Steps in Collecting* (London: T. Werner Laurie, 1913), pp. 295, 298–299.

15. *Peasant Art in Sweden, Lapland and Iceland,* edited by Charles Holme (London: The Studio, 1910), pp.11–12. The queen's name was Tyra Danabode.

16. Charles Holme, pp. 11–12 and illustrations no. 388, 389, 410–414, 429.

Chapter III

Marie Webster's principal source for this chapter was Margaret Jourdain, *English Secular Embroidery* (New York: E.P. Dutton & Co., 1912).

1. The Bayeux Tapestry is now believed to have been made in Normandy for William the Conqueror's half brother, Odo, Bishop of Bayeux, shortly after the Conquest. It is not actually a tapestry, but a strip of linen embroidered with colored wools in laid and couched work combined with outline stitches. See Mary Eirwen Jones, *A History of Western Embroidery* (London: Studio Vista, 1969), pp. 26–27.

2. The knight is also mentioned above on p. 18 and illustrated in Figure 5. (See Chapter II, note 2 and the note to Figure 5.) Webster's source was Jourdain, p. 9 and the illustration facing p. 8.

3. Jourdain, p. 10. Canterbury Cathedral, seat of the Archbishop, was founded in 597 A.D., but the present building dates from the 12th to the 15th centuries. St. Thomas à Becket was murdered there in 1170. In the Trinity Chapel is the magnificent tomb of Edward the Black Prince (son of Edward III), who died in 1376. His surcoat, which used to hang above the tomb, has been placed in the crypt and a replica displayed instead. It is embellished with his coat of arms: gold lions and fleurs-de-lis appliquéd onto crimson and blue velvet, and quilted with simple vertical lines. For a color photograph of the replica made at London's Royal School of Needlework in 1954, see Jones, Plate 14.

4. *Opus consutum:* see Chapter II, note 5.

Opus anglicanum, or "English work," refers to English ecclesiastical embroidery of the thirteenth and fourteenth centuries, renowned throughout Europe for its design and technique. Sacred figures appear against an elaborate architectural background; the stitchery is incredibly fine with extensive use of silk and gold. In addition to chain stitch, stem and split stitches were also used. A beautiful three-dimensional effect was produced by arranging the tiny stitches in a spiral pattern. (Jones, pp. 25–31, 154.)

5. For a description and illustration of this piece, known as "Saint Cuthbert's maniple and stole," see Barbara J. Morris, *English Embroidery* (Victoria and Albert Museum Illustrated Booklet, London: Her Majesty's Stationery Office, 1961), pp. 3, 13 and Plate 1. According to Morris, "this is the only English embroidery dating from before the Norman Conquest that has been preserved." It is of "linen, embroidered with coloured silks in split and stem stitches, and couched work in gold thread and red silk." Its Latin inscription reads, "Queen to Alfred's son and successor, Edward the Elder, was one Aelflaed, who caused this stole and maniple to be made for a gift to Fridestan consecrated Bishop of Winchester, A.D. 905." See Julia Addison, *Arts and Crafts in the Middle Ages* (London: G. Bell, 1908), p.199. Edward the Elder, Saxon king and son of Alfred the Great, ruled from 901 to 925 A.D.

6. Emily Leigh Lowes, *Chats on Old Lace and Needlework* (New York: Frederick A. Stokes, 1908), pp. 250–251. The ambitious Thomas Wolsey (ca. 1475–1530), Archbishop of York, Cardinal and Lord Chancellor of England under Henry VIII, set out in 1514 to build the largest house in England. In 1526, as his excessive power came under attack, Wolsey

presented Hampton Court to the king in a vain attempt to regain his favor.

7. Jourdain, p. 11. The quotation is out of context here; it was intended to refer to the fourteenth rather than to the sixteenth century.

8. See Addison, p. 197, whose source was probably Daniel Rock, *Textile Fabrics*, pp. 108–109:

> Small square pieces of embroidered linen are sometimes found in country houses in some old chest, of which the original use is said not to be now known. But in most cases these were made for children's quilts; and very often have the emblems of the evangelists figured at the corners: reminding us of the nursery rhyme, once common both in England and abroad—
> "Matthew, Mark, Luke, and John
> Bless the bed that I lie on."

Rock goes on to describe an adult-size quilt with the same design, found in the dormitory of the priory at Durham in 1446, which Addison mistakenly described as a "child's bedquilt." The emblems or symbols of the evangelists are: Matthew, angel; Mark, lion; Luke, bull; John, eagle.

The Squyr of Lowe Degre is quoted in Addison, p. 197, from the translation edited by William Edward Mead (Boston: Ginn & Co., 1904), p. 37.

9. Lowes, p. 360.

10. Lowes, p. 250. A tragic figure, Mary Queen of Scots (Mary Stuart) was born in 1542, the only child of James V of Scotland and the French noblewoman Marie de Guise. Mary succeeded to her father's throne when only six days old. She was sent to France to be educated at the Renaissance court of Henry II and his queen, Catherine de Medici. Mary was betrothed to their son, the future King Francis II, but he died only 17 months after their wedding. Mary, as a devout Roman Catholic, became a dangerous rival of her Protestant cousin, Queen Elizabeth I of England.

In 1561, Mary returned from France to rule Scotland, but in 1567 she was imprisoned by her Protestant nobles as a suspect in the murder of her second husband, Lord Darnley. She escaped to seek refuge in England, but Queen Elizabeth feared a plot and ordered the Earl of Shrewsbury to hold her prisoner, which he did for 18 long years. It was not until 1587 that Mary was finally tried and beheaded. Her only child, James Stuart, survived to rule both England, as James I, and Scotland, as James VI.

During her tedious years of confinement, one of Mary's favorite pastimes was needlework, often in the company of the spirited Countess of Shrewsbury (Elizabeth Hardwick), her jailer's wife. They copied designs of birds, animals and flowers from woodcuts and embellished them with monograms and cryptic mottoes. Embroidered emblems were sometimes appliquéd to velvet or other rich fabrics to make decorative bed hangings, valances and curtains, but professional embroiderers usually produced these large pieces. For a fascinating account of Mary's life and handiwork, see *The Needlework of Mary Queen of Scots* by Margaret H. Swain (New York: Van Nostrand Reinhold, 1973).

11. Jourdain, pp. 55–56. Hardwick Hall, a beautiful National Trust property in Derbyshire, houses an exceptional collection of Elizabethan furnishings and needlework. However, Mary Queen of Scots never stayed there, for it was built by the Countess of Shrewsbury after Mary's death. Although an improbably large number of embroideries has been attributed to Mary Queen of Scots, the only piece at Hardwick Hall now believed to be her handiwork is a monogrammed cushion embroidered in silk with the Scottish thistle, the English rose and the lily of France. Most of the surviving embroidery with Mary's initials can be seen at Oxburgh Hall, Norfolk, England. See Swain, pp. 95–96 and Helen Kelley, "Another Legend Laid to Rest," *Quilters' Journal,* Fall 1978, p. 19.

12. Jourdain, p. 54 and illustration facing p. 54.

13. Lowes, pp. 249–250 and Jourdain, p. 44.

14. Jourdain, pp. 50–51 and illustrations facing p. 48 and p. 50. The lady representing Faith and the Turk representing Heresy appear here in Figure 9.

15. Jourdain, p. 136. Katherine Howard (now generally spelled "Catherine"), was the fifth wife of King Henry VIII, whom he beheaded in 1542. Sarsenet was a thin silk fabric from Persia.

16. The quotation is from Lowes, pp. 284 and 287; see also Jourdain, pp. 24–25, 140–145. Catherine of Aragon (1485–1536), daughter of the Spanish monarchs Ferdinand and Isabella, was Henry VIII's first wife. When she proved unable to bear him a male heir, Henry divorced her and remarried, thus provoking the split with the Pope which led to the English Reformation. Many anecdotes about famous royal needlewomen were first collected in Chapter 24 of *The Art of Needlework,* edited by the Countess of Wilton (London: H. Colburn, 1840).

17. Lowes, pp. 287–288. In comparison with this fine 18th century work, Lowes, writing in 1908, deplored the English quilting of the mid-19th century, when the padding was placed "wholesale fashion ... between the sheets of cotton or linen, and a coarse back-stitching outlined in great scrawling patterns held the whole together."

18. Jourdain, p. 84. On the following page, Jourdain continues, "The pattern schemes of these beautiful and curious embroideries are doubtless derived from colour-printed cottons, 'palampores' from Masulipatam, where an agency was established in 1610–11, for the East India Company. Many of these palampores have remarkable tree and leaf patterns, composed of symmetrical interlacements of branches, bearing ornamental leaves, flowers, etc."

19. Lady Frances Parthenope Verney, *Memoirs of the Verney Family during the Civil War* (1892; reprint edition, New York: Barnes & Noble, 1970), Vol. 1, p. 293, quoted in Grace M. Vallois, *First Steps in Collecting* (London: T. Werner Laurie, 1913), pp. 22–23. The quotation from Lady Verney concludes, "This great black bed, with its impressive amplitude of gloom, travels about the family whenever a death occurs, till the very mention of it gives one a feeling of suffocation!"

This detailed history of one family at the time of the English Civil War was based on the papers of Sir Ralph Verney (1613–1696), "one of those useful men who seem to regard every scrap of written paper as sacred." Claydon House in Buckinghamshire was the family home.

20. The orange tree quilt is illustrated in Jourdain, facing p. 88, with the caption, "Quilt embroidered in coloured silks, representing a gentleman and lady (temp. William III) and an orange tree." William III shared the throne with Queen Mary II from 1689 to 1695, and then ruled alone until 1702.

Jourdain, p. 90, states, "There is an elaborate bed-quilt at Madresfield Court, said to have been worked by Anne (whilst Princess) and her friend Lady Marlborough." Queen Anne (1665–1714), the last of the Stuarts, reigned from 1702 until 1714. Her childhood friend was Sarah, later the Duchess of Marlborough, and the "wild, unmerciful house" full of quilts was Blenheim Palace. (See Vallois, pp. 29–31.) This enormous structure was a gift from the nation to Sarah's husband, John Churchill, the first Duke of Marlborough, as a reward for defeating the French in 1704. The Duchess found it too grandiose and quarreled with the architect, Sir John Vanbrugh, who left before his baroque masterpiece was finished. Lavishly furnished and decorated, Blenheim is also renowned as the birthplace of Sir Winston Churchill.

21. Jourdain, pp. 101–103. Mary Granville Delany, "The Great Mrs. Delany," was a notable character of her time, appreciated for her wit and style as well as for her intelligence and artistic talents. According to Lady Llanover, who edited her correspondence in 1861, Mrs. Delany probably started the white linen quilt in 1750, but never finished it. The other piece was not a quilt but a set of bed hangings made of nankeen, a sturdy and washable yellow cotton fabric: "The patterns were leaves united by bows of ribbon, cut out in white linen and sewed down with different varieties of *knotting* in white thread — which gave relief, and light, and shade." The workmanship and materials proved so durable that by Lady Llanover's time it had withstood a hundred years of continual use! See *The Autobiography and Correspondence of Mrs. Delany*, edited by Sarah Chauncey Woolsey (revised from Lady Llanover's edition of 1861; Boston: Little, Brown & Co., 1898), Vol. 1, pp. 264 and 374; Vol. 2, p. 488.

22. Quoted in Jourdain, p. 138. Edward Terry (1590–1660) traveled to India in 1616 as chaplain to Sir Thomas Roe, an ambassador sent by the king of England to wring trade concessions from the Great Mogul who ruled India. Terry's account of this journey was published in 1655 under the lengthy title, *A Voyage to East-India, Wherein Some Things are Taken Notice of in our Passage Thither, but Many More in our Abode There, Within that Rich and Most Spacious Empire of the Great Mogul*. These contacts paved the way for the English East India Company to import a colorful array of Indian printed cottons, forever changing English taste in fabrics.

23. Jourdain, pp. 61, 137–138.

24. Jourdain, pp. 112–114. Lady Mary Coke (1726–1811), daughter of the Duke of Argyll, was a rather pompous aristocrat who visited the extravagant Viennese court of the Hapsburg emperor, Joseph II, and his mother, Maria Theresa, in 1770, 1772 and 1773. See *The Letters and Journals of Lady Mary Coke* (1889–96; reprint edition, Bath: Kingsmead Reprints, 1970).

25. Section 22 of *Some Thoughts Concerning Education*, 1693. John Locke (1632–1704), British rationalist philosopher and political theorist, championed the principles of freedom and tolerance in his influential *Two Treatises of Government* (1690).

26. Samuel Pepys (1633–1703) kept his famous diary from 1660 to 1669. In 1655 he had married the fifteen-year-old daughter of French Protestant immigrants; but she fell ill and died before she was 30. He lived alone the rest of his life, a respected Admiralty official and even, on occasion, a member of parliament.

27. One of these quilted curtains is illustrated in Jourdain, facing p. 136.

28. Jourdain, p. 96. The witty Lady Mary Wortley Montagu (1689–1762) traveled to Constantinople with her husband, the British ambassador. Her letters, first published in 1763, have been described as "vivid, downright and scandalous," assuring them a wide readership. She is also remembered for having introduced into England the Turkish practice of inoculation against smallpox.

29. Jourdain, p. 96. The *Spectator* was a popular London paper published in 1711 and 1712 by Joseph Addison and Richard Steele. Their opinions were voiced by the fictional Mr. Spectator, a humorous observer of society, who frequented the popular coffee houses of the day. In this exchange on the decline of needlework, Mr. Spectator suggested the advantages of needlework over other occupations for ladies: "This is, methinks, the most proper way wherein a lady can shew a fine genius, and I cannot forbear wishing, that several writers of that sex had chosen to apply themselves rather to tapestry than rhyme. Your pastoral poetesses may vent their fancy in rural landscapes, and place despairing shepherds under silken willows, or drown them in a stream of mohair...." He then proposed several tongue-in-cheek statutes that "would effectually restore the decayed art of needlework, and make the virgins of Great Britain exceedingly nimble-fingered in their business," for example: "That no young Virgin whatsoever be allowed to receive the addresses of her first lover but in a suit of her own embroidering." (*Spectator*, No. 606, quoted in Jourdain, pp. 96–98.)

30. Quoted in Jourdain, pp. 107–108, from Catherine Hutton, *Reminiscences of a Gentlewoman of the Last Century* (Edited by Catherine Hutton Beale; Birmingham: Cornish Brothers, 1891), p. 213. Catherine Hutton, physically frail, but with a powerful intellect, was born in 1756 and lived to the age of 90. In 1846, near the end of her life, she wrote a detailed chronicle of her achievements, which included the publication of 12 volumes of fiction and history, and notable collections of costume prints and autographs. Her domestic accomplishments were equally impressive and included pastry making, gardening and many kinds of sewing: "I have made patchwork beyond calculation, from seven years old to eighty-five. My last piece was begun in November, 1840, and finished in July, 1841. It is composed of 1,944 patches, half of which are figured or flowered satin, of all colours, formed into stars; the other half is of black satin, and forms a ground work. Here ended the efforts of my needle."

31. See Jourdain, pp. 147–148. These mottoes are given as examples of the emblem work of the Elizabethan period; they embellished a piece of embroidery (not a quilt) from the sixteenth (not the seventeenth) century.

32. John Taylor, "The Praise of the Needle" (1640), in *Works of John Taylor, the Water Poet* (1870; reprint edition, New York: Burt Franklin, 1967), p. 3. John Taylor (1580–1653), was a boatman on the Thames and something of an eccentric. He wrote this delightful poem as an introduction to J. Boler's pattern book, "The Needle's Excellency." Taylor's list of the common needlework stitches of his day has been frequently quoted in embroidery books.

33. Elizabeth Glaister, *Needlework* (London: Macmillan, 1880), pp. 96–101, 104. This was part of the popular "Art at Home" series on topics of interest to the Victorian housewife, such as interior decoration, drawing and wood carving. It even included a volume on amateur theatricals, illustrated by Kate Greenaway.

Chapter IV

1. This statement, often repeated by later quilt historians, has been challenged by Sally Garoutte in her article, "Early Colonial Quilts in a Bedding Context," published in *Uncoverings 1980* (Mill Valley, CA: American Quilt Study Group, 1981), pp. 18–25. In her study of the period from 1620 to 1700, she found that the most common bedcoverings were woolen blankets and bed ruggs, while "quilts in the early colonial period were few and far between." They were luxury items of the merchant class and "were almost certainly imported rather than homemade." All of these were whole cloth quilts rather than pieced or patchwork (appliqué) quilts. Garoutte concluded, "Quilts were not common or ordinary articles in early colonial times. Far from it. They were both rare and expensive."

2. Alice Morse Earle, *Customs and Fashions in Old New England* (1893; reprint edition, New York: Scribner's, 1968), pp. 118–119.

3. Alice Morse Earle, *Home Life in Colonial Days* (New York: Macmillan, 1898) pp. 270–274. Earle was regarded as the foremost authority on colonial customs. Her erroneous opinion that patchwork quilts and quilting bees were as common in the colonial period as in the 19th century was perpetuated by Webster in this chapter.

Earle found the anecdote about the Lord Mayor's cloak in Gideon T. Ridlon, *Saco Valley Settlements and Families* (1895; reprint edition, Rutland, VT: Charles E. Tuttle, 1969), pp. 426–427.

4. Helen Evertson Smith, *Colonial Days and Ways* (New York: Century Co., 1900), p. 119, and Gertrude Lefferts Vanderbilt, *The Social History of Flatbush* (New York: D. Appleton, 1881), pp. 146–147.

5. Charles Burr Todd, *The Story of the City of New York* (New York: Putnam's, 1888), pp. 112–113. This section describes New Amsterdam when Peter Stuyvesant was governor, from 1647 until his defeat by the English in 1664.

6. Vanderbilt, p. 83. Flatbush is actually a section of Brooklyn, across the East River from Manhattan.

7. The pirate was Captain William Kidd (1645–1701). He sailed from New York about 1696, commissioned by the king to hunt pirates. After Kidd and his motley crew turned to piracy themselves, he was arrested, tried and hanged. The inventory of his household effects appears in Alice Morse Earle, *Colonial Days in Old New York* (1896; reprint edition, Port Washington, NY: Ira J. Friedman, 1962), pp. 102–103.

8. Thomas Fairfax (1693–1781), the sixth Baron Fairfax, was an English nobleman who owned vast tracts of land in Virginia. His estate, Belvoir, was only four miles from Mount Vernon; in 1748, he employed his young neighbor, George Washington, as a surveyor.

9. "Oil-boiled calico" referred to colorfast fabrics originally produced in the Middle East by a complicated process. The most popular color was known as "Turkey red." See Barbara Brackman, *Clues in the Calico* (McLean, VA: EPM Publications, 1989), p. 62.

10. Elizabeth Daingerfield, "Patch Quilts and Philosophy," *Craftsman,* August 1908, pp. 523–524. Elizabeth Daingerfield (1866–1951) broke new ground with her articles on Kentucky quilts and quilters in this *Craftsman* article and two others in *The Ladies' Home Journal* (July 1909 and February 1912). A member of a prominent horse-breeding family in Lexington, Kentucky, she befriended many mountain women in the course of her mission work in rural districts. After her father's death in 1913, she put aside her church work and writing to manage the family stud farm. She earned a reputation as one of the most experienced and skillful breeders of thoroughbreds in the country; among her famous charges was Man o' War. (*New York Times,* 11 Dec. 1951, p. 33.) Marie Webster corresponded with her in 1914 (see Chap. VI, note 1).

11. Eliza Calvert Hall, *Aunt Jane of Kentucky* (Boston: Little, Brown, 1907), pp. 74–75. This quotation forms part of the chapter entitled "Aunt Jane's Album," in which Aunt Jane airs her quilts and enjoys the

memories they evoke. Eliza Calvert Hall was the pseudonymn of Eliza Caroline Calvert Obenchain.

12. Quoted in Julia Henderson Levering, *Historic Indiana* (New York: Putnam's, 1916), p. 105, from an address given at Chicago's Abraham Lincoln Centre in 1906. Jenkin Lloyd Jones (1843–1918) was a famous Unitarian leader, a crusader for social reform and an immensely popular public speaker. His family had emigrated from Wales to Wisconsin in 1845, and his early life was spent in the struggle to wrest a farm from the virgin forest. The "grave in the wilderness" undoubtedly refers to that of his Uncle Jenkin, whose early death made a deep impression on the boy. During World War I, Jones' unpopular pacifist beliefs sharply curtailed his career and his name was all but forgotten. See Thomas E. Graham, ed., *The Agricultural Social Gospel in America: "The Gospel of the Farm" by Jenkin Lloyd Jones* (Lewiston, NY: The Edwin Mellen Press, 1986).

13. Levering, pp. 98–99.

14. Levering, p. 75.

15. Levering, pp. 203–204.

16. A hand-colored photograph of Indiana Wreath appeared as the frontispiece in the early editions of *Quilts*. Newly photographed for this edition, the quilt is still in beautiful condition. (Cover illustration, Plates 30 and 31.) For information about the quiltmaker, Elizabeth J. Hart, see Notes on the Illustrations.

17. "The Country Contributor" was the pen name of Juliet Virginia Humphries Strauss (1863–1918), whose regular columns appeared for many years in several newspapers as well as in *The Ladies' Home Journal*. While still a young aspiring journalist on her hometown paper in Rockville, Indiana, she met and married a junior editor named Isaac Strouse, who later became its publisher and editor. Juliet's independent spirit is shown by her refusal to accept the Americanized spelling of her married name; she always used the German spelling, "Strauss."

In 1903, she began to write a Saturday column under the name of "The Country Contributor" for the *Indianapolis News,* which led to an invitation from *The Ladies' Home Journal* to contribute a monthly column, "Ideas of a Plain Country Woman." Her straightforward and humorous writing won her such popularity that her early articles were collected into a book, *The Ideas of a Plain Country Woman* (New York: Doubleday, Page & Co., 1908). Her homespun philosophy emerged from her own experience of women's daily concerns and was generously laced with nostalgia for the old-fashioned virtues of thrift, hard work and cheerfulness in the face of domestic drudgery, all of which she exemplified in her own life.

Chapter V

1. Elizabeth Daingerfield, "Patch Quilts and Philosophy," *Craftsman,* August 1908, p. 524. See Chapter IV, note 10.

2. Lewis F. Day and Mary Buckle, *Art in Needlework* (London: B.T. Batsford, 1900), pp. 148, 150. This paragraph concludes with a comment on the status of appliqué in London at the turn of the century: "Of course, it is not popular."

3. This quilting design "from an Old English Quilt" was adapted from an illustration in Elizabeth Glaister, *Needlework* (London: Macmillan, 1880), p. 99. On p. 97, Glaister recommends it "for a small coverlet or the centre of a large one.... It is taken from a fragment of old work, done in rather thick yellow sewing silk on moderately fine linen, the centres in buttonhole stitch and the outlines in chain and other stitches; the circles of the original are about four inches across."

Chapter VI

1. Elizabeth Daingerfield, "Patch Quilts and Philosophy," *Craftsman,* August 1908, p. 527. In this article, the quiltmaker was called "Aunt Cynthia Steele." Daingerfield may have revealed this woman's true identity in a letter written to Marie Webster on October 19, 1914. Daingerfield mentioned "the mountain owner of 83 of her own quilts" from Breathitt County, Kentucky, a woman with "innumerable grandchildren... called 'Aunt Libbie Crawford' by all the community." Some of her quilts were probably among those illustrated in Daingerfield's two *Ladies' Home Journal* articles: "Kentucky Mountain Patchwork Quilts" (July 1909) and "The Kentucky Mountain Quilt" (Feb. 1912). See also Chap. IV, note 10.

2. Robert and Elizabeth Shackleton, *The Quest of the Colonial* (New York: Century Co., 1907), p. 202.

Chapter VII

1. The South Kensington Museum is now the Victoria and Albert Museum.

2. See Chapter VI, note 1.

3. Patrick Weston Joyce, *A Social History of Ancient Ireland* (1913; reprint edition, New York: Benjamin Blom, 1968), Vol. 2, pp. 441–444.

4. "The Country Contributor" was Juliet Strauss, of Rockville, Indiana (see Chapter IV, note 17). Marie Webster's scrapbook, now in the Indianapolis Museum of Art, contains an undated clipping from the *Indianapolis News* describing this show. Under a headline reading, "Quilt Contest Given: Prizes Awarded for Best Designs at Rockville Entertainment," was this report: "An unusual entertainment was given by the Woman's Civic League at the high school auditorium Saturday afternoon, under the direction of Mrs. Juliet V. Strauss, known as the Country Contributor.... The contest far exceeded expectations, for nearly one hundred and fifty quilts and counterpanes from Rockville and other parts of Parke County were exhibited." It was reported that there were several 100-year old quilts and one from Virginia thought to be 150 years old.

5. Harriet Beecher Stowe, *The Minister's Wooing* (New York: Derby & Jackson, 1859), pp. 248–249.

Chapter VIII

1. James G. M. Ramsey, *The Annals of Tennessee to the End of the Eighteenth Century* (1853; reprint edition, New York: Arno Press, 1971), p. 725.

2. Phebe Earle Gibbons, *"Pennsylvania Dutch" and Other Essays* (revised edition, 1882; reprint edition, New York: AMS Press, 1971), pp. 30–31.

3. Gibbons, p. 44.

4. Quilt historian Cuesta Benberry has observed that this is the earliest published reference to Hawaiian quilts. Marie Webster's interest in this subject led her to correspond with several women in Hawaii who sold her Hawaiian quilts. One of these, called Rain Falling in Honolulu, appeared as a black and white illustration in Doubleday's 1926 and 1928 editions of *Quilts* (Fig. 70).

5. Stowe, *The Minister's Wooing,* pp. 453–461.

List of Quilt Names

Cuesta Benberry has noted that Marie Webster's list of quilt names closely parallels the traditional patterns collected by the Ladies' Art Company of St. Louis, Missouri. This well-known pattern supplier, founded in 1889, published its early catalogs under the title, *Diagrams of Quilt, Sofa and Pin Cushion Patterns.* In the early 1900s, the catalog contained sketches of some 420 quilt patterns. Webster's list has 467 names, which includes most of the Ladies' Art Co. names, plus the names of all of her own designs completed by 1915: Bedtime; Bunnies; Daffodils and Butterflies; Daisies; Dogwood; French Baskets; Grapes and Vines; Iris; Morning Glory; Morning Glory Wreath; Pansies and Butterflies; Poppy; Rose; Snowflake; Sunbonnet Lassies; Sunflowers; Wild Rose; Wind-blown Tulips; Wreath of Roses. See Cuesta Benberry, "An Historic Quilt Document: The Ladies Art Company Catalog" in *Quilters' Journal,* Vol. 1, no. 4, Summer 1978, pp. 13–14.

List of References

This list contains many typographical errors. Corrected entries with full details of publication appear in the Bibliography, pp. 225–230.

NOTES ON THE ILLUSTRATIONS

Color Plates

Plates 1-14. These are the original color illustrations from *Quilts: Their Story and How to Make Them,* showing Marie Webster's designs which were published by *The Ladies' Home Journal* in 1911 and 1912. The captions in the book were adapted from the magazine articles.

Plates 1-4 illustrate the designs from *The Ladies' Home Journal* of January 1, 1911. However, by 1915, the original negatives were no longer available and new photographs were taken especially for the first edition of *Quilts.* The Wind-blown Tulip quilt with yellow flowers and butterflies that appeared in *The Journal* was replaced by another quilt in the same pattern, with pink flowers and no butterflies (Plate 4). Pink Rose, later called American Beauty Rose, was Marie Webster's first quilt and is now in the collection of the Indianapolis Museum of Art (Plate 1).

Plates 5-8 appeared in the January 1912 issue of *The Ladies' Home Journal.* Sunflower (Plate 8) is also in the Indianapolis Museum of Art, part of a gift of ten Marie Webster quilts from her daughter-in-law, Mrs. Gerrish Thurber. A detail is shown in Plate 18.

Plates 9-14 show the six baby quilts pictured in *The Ladies' Home Journal* in August 1912. Three of them are now in the Indianapolis Museum of Art: Daisies (Plate 12), Morning Glory Wreath (Plate 13) and Bedtime (Plate 14).

Plate 15. A page from *The Ladies' Home Journal* of August 1911, showing Marie Webster's appliqué cushion designs. The magazine's large format, 11 x 16 inches, greatly enhanced the impact of its color pages.

Plates 16-29. Additional Marie Webster designs, newly photographed for this edition.

Plates 30-36. New color photographs of some of the heirloom quilts illustrated in black and white in *Quilts.*

Black and White Illustrations

The first edition of *Quilts: Their Story and How to Make Them* was illustrated with 66 black and white photographs. Fortunately, Marie Webster saved the originals, which have been used in the production of this new edition. Because she wrote the name of the owner of the quilt on the back of some of the photographs, it has been possible to determine that at least 23 of the quilts belonged to friends who were living in or near Marion, Indiana, in 1915 (Figs. 11, 12, 15, 16, 18–21, 24, 30–33, 36–38, 40–42, 44, 45, 51, 61). Some of these quilts were probably brought from eastern states when their owners migrated westward in the 19th century, some were made in Indiana and a few, such as Tulip Tree Leaves (Fig. 36), were evidently purchased.

Four additional pictures showed quilts from Marie Webster's own family: Grapes and Vines (Fig. 66 and Plate 16), which she herself made in 1914; two silk quilts (Figs. 56 and 58) made by her mother, Minerva Lamoreaux Daugherty; and North Carolina Lily (Fig. 34 and Plate 32), believed to have been made by Marie's two aunts, Letitia and Elizabeth Jane Daugherty.

Two of the photographs showed scenes in the town of Marion. Quilts on a Line (Fig. 64) was taken in the Webster's backyard on South Washington Street; Old Ladies Quilting (Fig. 65), showing two local women at their quilting frame, was taken at the Emily Flinn Memorial Home on Valley Avenue.

Six more photos were obtained at quilt shows that Marie Webster attended in Indiana or neighboring states between 1912 and 1915, when she was working on the book. Exhibit labels, virtually illegible in the photos, can be seen pinned to the quilts and bedspreads in Figures 23, 26, 27, 35, 39 and 54.

Four of the illustrated quilts belonged to Emma B. Hodge of Chicago, who donated them in 1919 to the Art Institute of Chicago (Figs. 47, 48, 52, 55 and Plate 34). They also appeared in Elizabeth Wells Robertson, *American Quilts* (New York: The Studio Publications, 1948), pp. 126, 132–133, and in Mildred Davison, *American Quilts* (Chicago: The Art Institute of Chicago, 1966), Figs. 9, 21, 22, 28.

In 1926, Doubleday, Page & Co. brought out a new edition of *Quilts* which included four additional black and white illustrations. Three showed quilts from Madison, Wisconsin, where Marie Webster had been invited to lecture at a quilt show in 1917; she probably obtained the photographs at that time (Figs. 67–69). The fourth picture was of a Hawaiian quilt that Marie Webster purchased in 1916 from a woman who lived on the island of Kauai (Fig. 70). The 1928 printing of

196

Quilts was the last to include these four photographs, until the present edition.

Frontispiece. INDIANA WREATH. A hand-tinted copy of this photograph was used for the frontispiece of the early editions of *Quilts,* in 1915, 1916, 1926, 1928 and 1929. The quilt is still in excellent condition and was newly photographed to appear on the cover of this new edition and in Plates 30 and 31. Marie Webster's glowing description of the quilt appears on pp. 84–86, where she calls it "the very perfection of quilt making."

Indiana Wreath was made in 1858 by Elizabeth J. Hart (1825–1904) in Hartford City, Indiana, a town about 20 miles from Marion. Her family were early settlers of the area, having moved there in 1838 from Pennsylvania. Although Elizabeth never married, she raised a young cousin after his mother's death when he was only two. Known as "Aunt Libby" to her large circle of friends, she was said to be "unostentatious" and "an estimable woman in every way." (*Hartford City Evening News,* 31 Aug. 1904.)

The colored photograph of Miss Hart's quilt has inspired many excellent quilters to create their own interpretations of this challenging design. Rose Kretsinger made her masterpiece in 1927; it is now in the Spencer Museum of Art. Charlotte Jane Whitehill's exquisitely quilted example in the Denver Art Museum was made in 1930. (For illustrations, see two catalogs of quilt exhibits held in Japan: *American Patchwork Quilt,* The Denver Art Museum, 1986, Fig. 1, and *American Patchwork Quilt,* Spencer Museum of Art, University of Kansas, 1987, Plate 42.) The pattern for Indiana Wreath was published in *McCall's Needlework Magazine,* Winter 1937–38, p. 26. (Cuesta Benberry, personal communication.)

Figure 1. SECTION OF FUNERAL TENT OF AN EGYPTIAN QUEEN. This illustration was taken from Alan S. Cole, "Old Embroideries," Part 1, *Home Needlework Magazine,* July 1900, p. 174. Webster's description of the tent on p. 11 is based on the material in Cole, pp. 178–179. Fragments of the tent are in the collection of the Egyptian Museum, Cairo. (See also Chapter I, note 6.)

Figures 2, 3 & 4. MODERN EGYPTIAN PATCHWORK. These pieces probably belonged either to Marie Webster or to one of her friends, for she once dressed up in the colorful patchwork and posed for her photograph (Fig. 75).

197

Figure 5. OLD ENGLISH APPLIQUÉ This piece is described on pp. 18 and 35. The illustration was taken from Margaret Jourdain, *English Secular Embroidery* (New York: E. P. Dutton, 1912), facing p. 8. It is now believed to be an early 14th century example of *opus anglicanum,* the exquisite English embroidery of the Middle Ages. A fragment about 8 inches square, it is embroidered in silver and silver-gilt thread, embellished with colored silks. The embroidery has been cut away from its original background of green velvet and remounted at a later date. See Mary Eirwen Jones, *A History of Western Embroidery* (London: Studio Vista, 1969), Fig. 8, and the catalog from the Victoria and Albert Museum, *Opus Anglicanum* (London: The Arts Council, 1963).

Figure 6. FIFTH CENTURY APPLIQUÉ. This illustration appeared in Constance Cary Harrison, *Woman's Handiwork in Modern Homes* (New York: Scribner's, 1881), p. 60. It was described as a specimen of Venetian appliqué of the *cinquecento,* which is Italian for "the 1500s." Here it has been mistranslated as "fifth century," producing an error in the date of over one thousand years! According to Harrison,

> The scroll-patterns in the strip are cut from crimson velvet ornamented with spangles, and sewn with silk cording upon a ground of cloth of gold. The other portions of the design are of a beautiful pinkish-red color, in silk. The cushion-cover draped above it has a ground of royal purple velvet, with bands of lemon-yellow silk. The central design is of rich ivory-yellow silk, and the other patterns vary from deep to lighter greens. The tassels are of variegated silk and gold (pp. 59–60).

Figure 8. PERSIAN QUILTED LINEN BATH CARPET. This illustration was taken from Alan S. Cole, "Old Embroideries," Part 3, *Home Needlework Magazine,* January 1901, p. 8. Cole's description on pp. 9–11 was quoted by Webster on pp. 26–27 of *Quilts.* This bath or prayer rug from the Victoria and Albert Museum in London is actually made of cotton rather than linen. The ground is cream-colored (possibly discolored from white) and the silk embroidery is worked in tambour stitch. The flowers are white outlined in yellow with cerise centers, the stems are blue and the faded green leaves are outlined with a darker shade of blue. (Letter from Jennifer Wearden, Department of Textile Furnishings and Dress, Victoria and Albert Museum, 7 July 1989.)

This picture inspired master quiltmaker Pine Hawkes Eisfeller to make her famous Tree of Life quilt (1939). Appliquéd with multi-colored blossoms, it has been illustrated in color on the cover of *Quilters' Newsletter Magazine,* April 1982, and in *Twentieth Century Quilts, 1900–1950,* by Thomas K. Woodard and Blanche Greenstein (New York: E.P. Dutton, 1988), p. 49, Plate 41.

Figure 9. OLD ENGLISH HANGING WITH APPLIQUÉ FIGURES. This illustration, described by Webster on p. 44, was taken from Margaret Jourdain, *English Secular Embroidery* (New York: E.P. Dutton, 1912), facing p. 50, where it was captioned "Hanging of black velvet with appliqué ornament in coloured silks, representing a lady holding a book entitled 'Faith,' and a Turk reclining at her feet. Late sixteenth century. In the possession of the Duke of Devonshire, at Hardwick Hall." On p. 50, Jourdain remarks:

> The lady, closely resembling Queen Elizabeth in costume and feature, holds a cup in her left hand, and in her right a book bearing the word Faith; on her sleeve is the word Fides. At her feet reclines a Turk also holding a book on which is a word, now illegible. Above is a large panel with an oriental monarch beneath a canopy, with four courtiers in front.

Figure 10. OLD GERMAN APPLIQUÉ. This piece is in the collection of the Metropolitan Museum of Art, New York. It is an 18th century woolen patchwork cover, 43 x 57 inches, embroidered with equestrian and other figures surrounding a central medallion showing a hunter under a tree. The wool is in various brilliant colors and the details are worked in colored silk floss in herringbone, stem and chain stitches with a multi-colored fringe. It was purchased in 1909 from the collection of Baron Speck von Sternburg. (Letter from Danielle O. Grosheide, Assistant Curator, European Sculpture and Decorative Arts, Metropolitan Museum of Art, 18 October 1989.)

Figure 13. INTERIOR OF BEDROOM, COCHRAN RESIDENCE, DEERFIELD, MASS. This house is now owned by Historic Deerfield, Inc., and is used as the director's residence. According to the curator of Deerfield's Memorial Hall Museum, "the house previously belonged to Gertrude Cochran Smith, who made netted canopies, and the photograph shows a room she set up to display her canopies to the public." (Letter from Suzanne L. Flynt, Pocumtuck Valley Memorial Association, 15 Dec. 1989.)

Figure 22. WHITE QUILT WITH TUFTED BORDER. This is not a quilt but a woven coverlet, probably made near Manchester, England, in the town of Bolton, which specialized in this type of spread. Large numbers of Bolton coverlets were imported into the United States from the mid-18th century until well into the 19th century. This example is marked in loops with the inscription "PA & Co J2 C." (Letter from Amelia Peck, Assistant Curator, Department of American Decorative Arts, Metropolitan Museum of Art, 31 October 1989.)

Figure 23. SUNBURST AND WHEEL OF FORTUNE. The caption here is puzzling, for the exhibit label pinned to the Sunburst quilt states that it was made about 1850. Even in 1915, that could hardly be considered "a comparatively modern" quilt! The owner resided in Terre Haute, Indiana.

Figure 25. OLD BED AND TRUNDLE BED. The Memorial Hall Museum in Deerfield, Massachusetts, still displays a "colonial bed-chamber" with many of the same furnishings. The pieced hexagon quilt top was made ca. 1814 by three sisters, Mary, Persis and Polly Sheldon, aunts of George Sheldon, who founded the museum. A large quilt (98 x 100 inches), it is said to contain 4,705 pieces. The background is of beige linen, with brown, blue and red prints. (Letter from Suzanne L. Flynt, Curator of the Memorial Hall Museum, 15 Dec. 1989.)

Figure 26. TWO WHITE TUFTED BEDSPREADS. The spread on the right bears an exhibit tag stating that it was made in 1826.

Figure 27. TUFTED BEDSPREAD WITH KNOTTED FRINGE. Like Figures 23 and 26, this spread was apparently on display in Terre Haute, Indiana, when it was photographed. The label states that it was made in the Carolinas.

Figure 28. UNKNOWN STAR. This quilt was the source for some of the quilting designs shown on p. 108.

Figure 34. NORTH CAROLINA LILY. (83 x 99 inches.) A detail is illustrated in Plate 32. This is a quilt from the Daugherty family homestead near Treaty, just outside Wabash, Indiana. It is thought to have been made by Elizabeth Jane ("Jennie") and Letitia ("Letty"), sisters of Marie Webster's father, Josiah Daugherty, as a gift for their mother, Elizabeth Kraps Daugherty. Letty was born in 1837 and married in 1865. Jennie was two years younger; she married in 1868 and died giving birth to her first child a year later. If the sisters did indeed make the quilt, Webster's date, "more than 80 years old," i.e. before 1835, is about 25 years too early.

Figure 35. FEATHER STAR WITH APPLIQUÉ. This quilt served as the inspiration for Catherine Hamburger's quilt, Harlequin, which won a prize in the 1942 Woman's Day National Needlework Contest and was published in *Woman's Day* magazine in March 1943. (Cuesta Benberry, personal communication.)

Figure 40. SINGLE TULIP. (85 x 98 inches.) A detail from this quilt is shown in Plate 35. It belonged to friends of the Websters in Marion, Indiana.

Figure 42. ROSE OF SHARON. Dolores Hinson published a pattern based on this illustration in *A Quilter's Companion* (New York: Arco Publishing, 1973), p. 163.

Figure 43. ORIGINAL FLORAL DESIGNS. (78 x 90 inches.) This quilt, also shown in Plate 33, is now in the collection of the Vigo County Historical Society, Terre Haute, Indiana. It was donated by Mrs. Reid Ross, wife of the great-great-grandson of the maker, Mrs. McCasson, who appliquéd the top in 1844. It was quilted in 1910.

Figure 44. CONVENTIONAL TULIP. Dolores Hinson based one of her patterns on this illustration (*A Quilter's Companion,* p. 154). The four-block set was popular in the mid-19th century. See Barbara Brackman, *Clues in the Calico* (McLean, VA: EPM Publications, 1989), p. 126.

Figure 47: POINSETTIA. (83 x 84 inches.) This quilt, believed to date from about 1850, was part of the extensive collection belonging to Mrs. Emma B. Hodge of Chicago, which was given to the Art Institute of Chicago in 1919. Red blossoms and green foliage were appliquéd onto a white cotton ground; the flower tops and the pieced sawtooth border were made from a figured blue calico. The pattern was published in Hinson, *A Quilter's Companion,* p. 184.

Figure 48. WHIG ROSE. (76 x 82 inches.) This quilt, also known as Pumpkin Blossom, was made about 1848 by Mrs. George F. Gale and was donated by Emma B. Hodge to the Art Institute of Chicago. (A color photograph, courtesy of the museum, appears in Plate 34.) According to Mildred Davison, "the appliqué pattern is carried out in plain green, red, and yellow calico with accents of embroidery. The irregular quilting was done on the first Howe sewing machine brought into Washtenaw County, Michigan, and the birds and flower centers are thickly padded. There is a small pocket on the reverse side stamped 'Geo. F. Gale,' which is said to have been made for hiding gold pieces" (Davison, Fig. 22). Elias Howe patented his horizontal needle sewing machine in 1846 (Brackman, p. 100).

Figure 51. ORIGINAL ROSE DESIGN. Also shown in Plate 36, this quilt was made by Mary Elizabeth Secrist Ammons (ca. 1840–1911), whose family were early settlers of Marion, Indiana, arriving by covered wagon from Ohio in 1843. Her mother died soon after the move, so she and her sister were raised by an aunt. Her sister, Sarah Elma Secrist Charles, was also a fine quiltmaker; two of her quilts were illustrated in *The Romance of the Patchwork Quilt in America* by Carrie A. Hall and Rose G. Kretsinger (1935; reprint edition, New York: Bonanza Books), pp. 199–200.

Figure 52. PINEAPPLE DESIGN. (72 x 82 inches.) Made about 1852, this is one of the quilts given by Mrs. Emma B. Hodge to the Art Institute of Chicago. According to Mildred Davison, "The pattern is in plain red and green calico appliquéd on twenty-one blocks. The quilting is done in floral designs and square diamonds. The pineapple was the domestic emblem of hospitality and one of the most popular of all post-Colonial designs" (*American Quilts*, Fig. 28).

Figure 54. ROSE OF LEMOINE. The partially legible label in the corner identifies this as a "Tulip Quilt," which was appliquéd in 1857 and quilted later by the maker's daughter.

Figure 55. CHARTER OAK. (71 x 72 inches.) This is a quilt top from the Emma B. Hodge Collection, now in the Art Institute of Chicago. It is made up of nine blocks with oak trees and oak leaf variations in tan and blue printed calico, with a border of trees and eagles (Davison, Fig. 9). This design was stamped on the cover of the 1915, 1916, 1926, 1928 and 1929 editions of *Quilts: Their Story and How to Make Them*.

Figure 56. PUFFED QUILT OF SILK. This comforter was made in Wabash, Indiana, about 1900, by Marie Webster's mother, Minerva Lamoreaux Daugherty (1836–1922).

Figure 58. ROMAN STRIPE. (Pieced and tied, 62 x 72 inches.) This silk comforter was also made at the turn of the century by Minerva Daugherty. It is now in the collection of the Indianapolis Museum of Art.

Figure 59. AMERICAN LOG CABIN. Barn Raising variation. The Log Cabin pattern was introduced in the 1860s, using the new "pressed patchwork" technique, in which the pieces were sewn to a foundation block, starting in the center and working out (Brackman, pp. 99–100, 144, 146).

Figure 64. OLD LADIES QUILTING. This photograph was taken at the Emily Flinn Memorial Home and shows a resident (left) and Nancy Ellis Jay Helm (right), superintendent of the home from 1905 to 1920, at their quilting frame. This is probably the same frame that was used for quilting Marie Webster's quilts before they were photographed for *The Ladies' Home Journal* articles of 1911 and 1912. According to June R. McKown in *Marion: A Pictorial History* (St. Louis: G. Bradley Publishing, 1989, p. 27), "Mrs. Helm was a noted seamstress, who along with other members of the Twentieth Century Club, at the turn of the century, used needlework to provide funds for various local philanthropic projects." (Photo courtesy of Jean Coffman).

Figure 65. QUILTS ON A LINE. Marie Webster's Poppy quilt (Plate 5) and a Double Irish Chain are being aired in the Webster's back yard in Marion. This photograph provided the inspiration for the logo used on the title page of *Quilts* and also on Marie Webster's pattern envelopes and catalogs. (See Fig. 79.)

Figure 66. GRAPES AND VINES. Marie Webster designed and made this quilt in 1914, using linen for the appliqué (Plate 16). It is now in the Indianapolis Museum of Art.

Figures 67, 68 and 69. THREE QUILTS FROM MADISON, WISCONSIN. These appeared only in the 1926 and 1928 Doubleday editions of *Quilts*. The pictures were probably obtained in 1917, when

203

Marie Webster lectured at a quilt show in Madison, described by the *Madison Democrat* on April 26, 1917:

> Something entirely new to Madison in the way of art exhibits is the quilt show which opened at the Congregational church yesterday. Old quilts, some dating back as far as 1794; historic quilts, with such contrasting legends as Sherman's march to the sea, and the first landing of missionaries on the Sandwich Isles; and quilts of modern making, are gathered together for the first time and afford graphic illustration of the progress in the industry.
>
> Besides the exhibition of home articles, Miss Marie Webster, one of the foremost authorities in the art of quiltmaking, has several of her products on view, as well as patterns for them.... It was her book that gave impetus to the women of the Congregational church to get up the show.

Figure 70. THE RAIN FALLING IN HONOLULU. This illustration also appeared only in the 1926 and 1928 editions of *Quilts*. Marie Webster purchased the red and white Hawaiian quilt in 1916 from Dora Rice Isenberg, daughter of a prominent sugar planter and wife of the Lutheran pastor in Lihue on the island of Kauai. In her letter of May 22, 1916, Mrs. Isenberg asked to be paid for the quilt with $10 worth of books and patterns, rather than in cash:

Dear Mrs. Webster,

> I am sending you a quilt, an old one — "the rain falling in Honolulu." This design was first made in Honolulu, then taken to Maui, afterwards brought to Kauai. New quilts cost from $20 upwards; it was hard to get this one for the Hawaiians are ashamed to sell old ones. It has Hawaiian wool in it as lining — so many of the new ones have only cotton batting. Will you pay me the $10 in one of your books, DeLuxe Edition for $5, 1 book for $2.50 & the rest in patterns. I will send you also the information that I have gotten about quilts as soon as I have time. I had no idea how much poetical fancy and sentiment that had developed or had been taken over from their Tapas. Have the quilt washed & disinfected.

> Yours truly

> Dora R. Isenberg

[P.S.] The Hawaiians have a different name for the rain falling on each island.

MARIE WEBSTER: HER STORY

by

Rosalind Webster Perry

MARIE D. WEBSTER
This elegant portrait was taken in Marion, Indiana, about 1905.

FIGURE 71

MARIE WEBSTER: HER STORY

When Marie Webster pioneered the study of quilt history, she little dreamt that someday she herself would be recognized as one of its major figures. Her achievements were impressive for a woman of her generation, growing up at a time of rigid Victorian strictures. Her independent spirit led her to embark on a career as designer and author, when the twentieth century's first quilt revival provided the opportunity for her to develop her talents to the full.

This remarkable woman's life spanned an entire century of rapid change, from the Civil War to the dawn of the Space Age. She was born on July 19, 1859, in Wabash, a small town in rural northern Indiana, the eldest of the six children of Minerva Lumaree and Josiah Scott Daugherty, whose families had migrated westward from Ohio about 1850 to establish farms in the Wabash River Valley.

Josiah Daugherty was a born entrepreneur. As a young man, he started a profitable business venture with John Lumaree, his future father-in-law, shipping agricultural products to eastern cities. He joined a banking partnership and became bank president for thirty years, while engaging in many other enterprises, ranging from a furniture factory to a cattle ranch in New Mexico. He was one of Wabash's leading citizens, serving on the town council, the board of education and even as fire chief.

But Josiah also had an adventurous streak and a yearning for the frontier. In 1871, he joined the Hayden expedition of the United States Geological Survey, charged with exploring Yellowstone's volcanic wonders. Thanks to their pioneering report, this unique region won protection as America's first national park. One of its most spectacular features, "Minerva Terrace," was named by Josiah in honor of his wife.

Far less is known about Minerva's life. Proud of her French Huguenot ancestry, she dropped the Americanized spelling of the family name in favor of the original "Lamoreaux." An accomplished needlewoman, she passed these skills along to her daughters, along with the pioneer values of thrift, hard work and "making yourselves useful." She was also musically inclined and owned the first piano in town.

Their daughter Marie received her only formal education in the Wabash public schools. An outstanding student, she was chosen to deliver the salutatory address at her high school graduation in 1878. Her desire to go away to college was thwarted by illness, a mysterious "eye disease," which later was diagnosed as severe hay fever. Ironically, apart fom her allergies, Marie proved to be anything but frail, outliving all her younger brothers and sisters to reach the age of 97!

Undaunted by her failure to attend college, she embarked on a lifelong process of self education. She persuaded her parents to engage the local Catholic priest, Father Hallinan, a man of considerable learning, to tutor her in Greek and Latin. She was a voracious reader of literature, travel and history, and even tried her hand at journalism, writing and editing for the local newspaper.

A fashionable and witty young woman, with auburn hair and sparkling hazel eyes, Marie's lively personality and slender good looks attracted many admirers. George Webster, a young businessman from the nearby town of Marion, fell under her spell when she appeared in a Fourth of July parade, dressed as "Columbia." It was love at first sight!

Their wedding, on Saint Valentine's Day in 1884, was the social event of the season. Two hundred elegantly attired guests attended the lavish reception at the Daugherty home which followed a simple ceremony in the Presbyterian church. The newly-weds set off on a honeymoon through the south, with Mardi Gras in New Orleans as the high point of the trip.

After a few years in Chicago, the couple moved back to Marion, George's hometown, then a rapidly growing manufacturing center. They lived there for the remainder of their

MARIE DAUGHERTY
Marie Webster as a child, photographed about 1862, when she was
three years old.

FIGURE 72

FOUR GENERATIONS

Marie Webster holding baby Lawrence, photographed in 1885 with her mother, Minerva Lamoreaux Daugherty (right), and Minerva's mother, Emma Brooks Lumaree (center).

FIGURE 73

fifty-four years of married life, raising one son, Lawrence. George Webster, like his father-in-law, entered the banking profession and was highly regarded in the community. Active on the school and library boards, he played the church organ and was known for his generosity and delightful sense of humor. Marie always loved to travel, even during the early years of her marriage when her son was small. In 1891, she spent several months on her father's cattle ranch on the northern New Mexico frontier, at a time when bears and wolves still roamed the hills. At last, in the clean dry air of the high plains, she was free from allergies. She assumed the duties of ranch house cook, staying on with her father for the fall round-up. When they left to go home in December, a sudden blizzard overtook them on the way to the railroad station and they nearly froze to death, as their horses floundered in the snowdrifts. After surviving this adventure, Marie was content with more conventional travels: a visit to the celebrated 1893 World's Columbian Exposition in Chicago and a Grand Tour of Europe in 1899 to England, Holland, Germany, Switzerland and Italy.

Back in Marion, she settled down to a comfortable life, filled with family gatherings and social activities, amateur dramatics, club and volunteer projects. Reading and sewing were favorite pastimes. She was an expert needlewoman, having embroidered household and personal linens since she was a child. But it was 1909 — the year she turned fifty — before she made her first quilt.

The new century had ushered in a revival of quiltmaking. At a time of wrenching social change in America, nostalgia for a simpler era was sweeping the country and colonial-style furnishings were all the rage. *Craftsman* magazine popularized the ideas of the Arts and Crafts movement, advocating bold and simple designs, honestly expressed in natural materials. Handicrafts flourished in reaction to the tasteless machine-made products of the Victorian era and handmade quilts lent a "colonial" look to bedrooms across the land.

Marie Webster took up quiltmaking with enthusiasm. Since geometric pieced quilts were not to her taste, she decided to work out her own design. Inspired by a traditional Rose of

Sharon pattern, she appliquéd petals cut from soft shades of linen, adding a graceful curving trellis to unify the design. By quilting around each leaf and flower, she created a stunning three-dimensional effect.

Working with tiny stitches and her usual attention to detail, Marie had produced a masterpiece! Her friends and family were so enchanted with the quilt that they urged her to send it to *The Ladies' Home Journal*, which welcomed readers' new ideas.

Under the dynamic leadership of Edward Bok, *The Ladies' Home Journal* had become the most popular women's magazine in the country. As editor from 1889 to 1919, Bok was a tireless crusader for progressive social causes and was always airing new ideas, whether in fashion, home decoration, or on the controversial topics of the day. He aimed to improve the taste of his readers by vigorously promoting the Arts and Crafts ideal of simple good design.

The Journal was in the forefront of the quilt revival. It ran articles on "old patchwork" as early as the 1880s and at the turn of the century, commissioned a series of original designs by well-known artists like Maxfield Parrish and Jessie Willcox Smith. In 1908 and 1909, features by Mrs. Leopold Simon and Elizabeth Daingerfield stimulated interest in traditional quilts.[1]

Color printing was also pioneered by *The Journal*. Its color covers were among the first in the industry and in the fall of 1910, it delighted its readers with another innovation: full color on its fashion and needlework pages. Circulation soared and by year's end had grown to a million and a half, the largest in the nation.

When Marie Webster's Pink Rose quilt arrived in the magazine's Philadelphia office, it quickly caught Bok's eye. Recognising her talent, he invited her to submit more designs for a color feature on quilts — another first for *The Journal*.

Surprised and flattered, she accepted the challenge. Seeking inspiration in her garden, she gathered flowers, dried and pressed them, then traced their shapes. As she arranged and rearranged them, patterns began to emerge. She cut gracefully contoured patches from pastel linen, capturing the natural beauty of each kind of flower. When the hand appliqué work was finished, she took the tops to the Flinn Memorial Home, a women's residence nearby, to have them quilted with her original designs.[2]

The Ladies' Home Journal of January 1, 1911, featured photographs of four of her quilts in dazzling color: Pink Rose, Snowflake, Iris and Wind-blown Tulip (Plates 1–4). Delivered on Christmas Eve to homes across the country, this "New Year's Number" created a sensation. Marie Webster became a national celebrity overnight!

Fame, as she soon discovered, had its price. Beneath the quilts had appeared these fateful words: "NOTE: Transfer patterns cannot be supplied for any of these four quilts, but Mrs. Webster will be glad to answer inquiries regarding them if a stamped, addressed envelope is supplied." Inundated by requests for patterns, she enlisted her family and friends to cope with the crisis. Her 25-year-old son, Lawrence, a mechanical engineer, hit upon the idea of blueprinting the patterns. Instruction sheets were printed and full size mock-ups of the quilt blocks and borders were assembled by hand from colored tissue paper. Within a month, patterns for Marie Webster's "New Patchwork Quilts" were on sale for 50 cents apiece.

Invitations to exhibit the quilts soon followed. They were put on display at Marshall Field and Company, Chicago's most fashionable store. Even before the exhibit had opened to the public, "everything halted in the fancy goods department while employees flocked about the striking creations which represent a new development in artistic handiwork." They were a hit with the customers, too, spurring sales of patterns and fabric alike.[3]

The Ladies' Home Journal planned an ambitious series of Webster features, all in color. "The New Patchwork Cushions" appeared in August 1911, followed by "The New Flower Patchwork Quilts" in January 1912, which included a Sunflower quilt made at Bok's request. (See Plates 5–8, 15, 18.)

Last came "The Baby's Patchwork Quilt," in August 1912 (Plates 9–14). Marion Wire, editor of the needlework section, had asked Marie to "please let me have some of your literary work on this page, as well as your designs." So she submitted text as well as quilts. "Children," she wrote, "while very young show marked preference for certain toys and little belongings, and could they have pretty quilts for their very own they would surely love them dearly." The four floral quilts were very well received, but the two figurative quilts, Bedtime and Keepsake, stole the show. Keepsake with its "Sunbonnet Lassies" — stylish young women with gowns, bonnets and parasols made from treasured fabric scraps — would later evolve into the perennial favorite, Sunbonnet Sue.[4]

While making these quilts for *The Journal*, Marie had developed into a confident designer, always ready to try new ideas. She started out using a conventional square block format in her quilts, but soon broke free and experimented with blocks of many shapes and sizes, as in Poppies, Sunflowers and Daisies. Although her first quilt, Pink Rose, had an old-fashioned border and traditional quilting, her next three quilts — Iris, Snowflake and Wind-blown Tulip — introduced the imaginative borders and quilting motifs that would become her trademark. Shadowy quilted iris, snowflakes or tulips echoed the appliqué motifs, while snowdrifts or blossoms swirled around the edges of the quilts. In Iris, she boldly merged the flowers across block boundaries, forming a strong secondary pattern.

Her cushion designs were also important, for they contained the seeds of many of her later quilt motifs (Plate 15). Elements from two pillows, Wild Rose Wreath and Rose Vine, were later combined to form her famous Wreath of Roses quilt, published in *The Journal* in 1915 (Plate 21). Another cushion showed the field daisy, which reappeared in the Daisy baby quilt (1912) and French Baskets with Daisies (1914). Yet another design featured a quilted spider web, also used in the Sunflower quilt.

She allowed her imagination full play in her 1912 *Journal* quilts. Looking at each one as a picture within a frame, she began to use the old medallion style, out of favor since the mid-nineteenth century. To focus attention on the middle, she reserved an open area for the display of intricate quilting designs, seen in her Sunflower, Dogwood and Morning Glory

FAMILY PORTRAIT

Marie Webster (left) with her brothers and sisters — Karl, Lucy, Emma and Lawrence Daugherty — and her husband, George Webster, seated (right) with son Lawrence. Photographed in Wabash, Indiana, in 1889.

FIGURE 74

EGYPTIAN PATCHWORK

Marie Webster dressed in a costume made from the Egyptian patchwork panels and cushion covers shown in Figures 2, 3 and 4.

FIGURE 75

patterns, as well as some of her baby quilts, like Keepsake, Morning Glory Wreath and Wild Rose (Plates 6-8, 10, 11, 13).

It would be hard to overestimate the revolutionary impact of Marie Webster's fourteen *Ladies' Home Journal* quilts on modern quilt design. They introduced a fresh new naturalism to the art of appliqué and created a fashion for solid pastel colors that persisted well into the 1930s. The popularity and status of *The Journal* had made Marie Webster the nation's first quilt celebrity, which soon led to an offer to write a book on the subject.

Doubleday, Page & Co. was the fastest growing publishing house in the country. Thanks to the enterprise of its founder and publisher, Frank Doubleday, it was "the wonder of the publishing world," with books by famous writers like Kipling, Conrad and Upton Sinclair on its list. An innovator in all aspects of the business, Doubleday, Page promoted its titles vigorously through mail order, advertising and its own chain of bookstores.

Frank Doubleday was a good friend of Edward Bok. It seems likely that the two men discussed the growing public interest in the revival of American handcrafts and the phenomenal success of Marie Webster's *Journal* features. In 1912, Doubleday invited her to write a history of quilts appealing to a general audience as well as to needlewomen and collectors of antiques.

Marie Webster eagerly accepted the offer. As a student of history, she relished the challenge of unearthing the origins of quiltmaking and tracing its development. When she had exhausted the resources of the local library, she went to visit her son in Cleveland and continued her work in the city library. She read her way along the history shelves, from ancient Egypt to colonial America, searching for any passing mention of appliqué or quilting. She turned to needlework books for examples of medieval, Elizabethan and Victorian patchwork and even consulted a ten-volume study of ancient art — in French! On the lighter side, novels like Harriet Beecher Stowe's *The Minister's Wooing* and Eliza Calvert Hall's *Aunt Jane of Kentucky* provided colorful anecdotes.

Doubleday planned to illustrate the book with color pictures of the author's fourteen quilts from her *Journal* articles. Marie Webster assembled 67 black-and-white illustrations and hand-colored one of them, Indiana Wreath, for the frontispiece. Although a few pictures were obtained from books, museums and collectors, she arranged most of the photography herself. When she went to exhibitions, she took a photographer along and also had him take pictures of the finest quilts belonging to her friends. Never before had so many quilt photographs been gathered together.

Busy as she was with the book, Marie still found time to make quilts. Between 1912 and 1915, she created five new designs: Grapes and Vines; French Baskets with Daisies; Daffodils and Butterflies; Bunnies; Wreath of Roses. Grapes and Vines was her most intricate pattern, with each grape individually appliquéd from a separate piece of purple linen (Plate 16). French Baskets included reverse appliqué on a ground of pale blue gingham, marking a shift away from linen toward lighter weight cotton. Bunnies was the last of her children's quilts, a delightful design of white Easter rabbits and baskets brimming with brightly colored eggs (Plates 19 and 20). The last of this group was a fresh interpretation of an old favorite, Wreath of Roses, shown in October 1915 in *The Ladies' Home Journal* (Plate 27).

The quilt craze hit its peak in the fall of 1915, when the United Press issued this tongue-in-cheek dispatch:

> Good gracious, can it really be
> This season that we're going to see
> The good old-fashioned quilting bee
> Replace the favored tango tea?
> It certainly looks so to me!

> The newest bee in milady's bonnet is a mighty old one — the quilting bee, if you please. At least, a perfect passion for this old time handwork is sweeping over the modern hearth and now no home is complete without a bit of handsome quilting.[5]

Just a few weeks later, on October 28, 1915, *Quilts: Their Story and How to Make Them* was published. Doubleday issued two versions: a "deLuxe" limited edition of 125 numbered copies which cost $5.00 and a standard edition for $2.50. The deLuxe was a truly elegant volume, larger and more lavish than the standard, specially boxed and edged in gold. The Websters were so pleased with the handsome appearance of the book that both Marie and her son wrote letters of congratulation to the publisher. Russell Doubleday, Frank's brother, replied to Marie (who was enjoying a well-deserved vacation in California), "We are proud of it in this office. We have heard many nice things about it, and we believe the sale is going to be satisfactory. It is a pleasure to issue so distinguished a book." To Lawrence he wrote, "I believe it will sell well; although it is not the sort of book that will have a large sale all at once." In spite of this note of caution, it sold so well that it went into a second printing within a year.

Like all of Doubleday's books, *Quilts* was promoted aggressively. It was in the bookstores just in time for Christmas and was widely reviewed as an ideal gift selection. For example, the *Philadelphia Public Ledger* gave it this warm endorsement:

> To the ordinary unenlightened reader this book will prove a perfect revelation, for it is astonishing how much of interest and romance the author has succeeded in weaving round an apparently commonplace subject.... This volume would make a very charming gift for a housewifely woman, and even in these strenuous days there are, thank goodness, quite a number left.

Altogether, an impressive list of 24 publications reviewed the book, including the *New York Times, New York Sun, New York Herald* and *New York Evening Post*; in Boston, the *Herald Transcript* and *Christian Science Monitor*; in the Midwest, the *Indianapolis News* and the *Chicago Tribune,* as well as many local papers. It was even mentioned in *Life* magazine. The trend-setting *Craftsman* magazine found it "thoroughly delightful . . . one of the most attractive of the recent handcraft books. Every New Englander, collector, antiquarian should possess this book."

Since a leaflet advertising her patterns was inserted in every book, the author was swamped by a tidal wave of orders and letters of congratulation from all over the country and around the globe — England, Finland, India, China, New Zealand, Australia and Hawaii. By the time the second printing sold out in 1919, she had received over 6,000 pieces of mail.

Only a month after *Quilts* appeared, *Who's Who in America* requested her to "kindly furnish data for a brief personal sketch of yourself." Women's achievements were still so rarely recognized that the form letter they sent her began, "Dear Sir," which had been crossed out and replaced by "Dear Madam."

Letters of appreciation arrived from several quilt dealers, like the proprietor of "The Quilting Bee," a shop in Rye, New York, and Katharine Willis from Long Island, who found the book "of great value to me in my business. Every new quilt I get in I always go at once to your book to see if it is 'In the book.'" (She then offered to sell a rare documented Revolutionary period quilt for the princely sum of $12.00.)

Marie Webster also heard from collectors like George Ketcham of Toledo, Ohio, a wealthy horse breeder who was famous for his trotting horse Cresceus, "the fastest in the world." He wrote, "The thought occurs that you may know of some new or old quilts for sale. I have a modest collection, and am always desirous of adding good specimens to same." He had been purchasing quilts from another horse breeder, Elizabeth Daingerfield, the author of several articles on Kentucky mountain quilters. Discovering that some of these quilters welcomed commissions, Ketcham asked Miss Daingerfield to have all Marie Webster's patterns made up in Kentucky for his collection.[6]

From the British Isles came two especially interesting letters. Marie Corelli, author of *A Romance of Two Worlds* and *Sorrows of Satan*, was England's most popular novelist when she wrote, "I daresay you know my name as the author of many books; I began so young and have written so much that people think I must be quite old! — but I'm glad to say such is not the case!" Her enthusiastic order for a baby quilt pattern requested "full instructions — yes, please! — very full! — for I am a beginner at this... and would love to try my hand, under your guidance."

The Countess of Lisburne in Wales was one of several people who ordered patterns for their benevolent projects. In 1918, she wrote about the cottage industry she was setting up in Cardiganshire: "In the old days Wales was famous for its quilting, but I am sorry to say that the art has been dying out in the last few years, and now only a few very old women remember how to work quilts.... I am making an effort to revive this old work, and I am glad to say that my effort is so far proving most successful. I have over twenty quilters employed at present and the work they are producing is, I consider, quite as good as the old."

American social reformers also embraced the quilt revival as a means of helping impoverished families. A philanthropic New York businessman wrote to Marie Webster, "Up to now the chief thought has been to get these poorer women into plain sewing of a commercial character but I don't see why they couldn't make just as much money (or as 'little' would more properly describe it!) and a lot more enjoyment working on quilts than pushing a machine on shirts or overalls." Meanwhile, the Citizens' Employment Bureau of Indianapolis devised a project "to be devoted exclusively to the piecing and quilting of quilts." Their motto was "a quilt for every home," to be made by "refined women who have never before worked outside their own homes, but who are willing to practice their art to help in the support of their families until their husbands obtain employment."

Dr. William Rush Dunton, Jr., a pioneer in the field of occupational therapy, ordered patterns for his Maryland hospital program. Delighted with his patients' response, he wrote, "If you had been on the ward with me this morning and seen the group of ladies who are engaged in making your wind blown tulip I think you will realise that we have already succeeded in arousing some interest." When he told Marie about a quilt exhibit he was planning at the hospital, she sent him some of her quilts. Dr. Dunton pursued this interest, becoming an expert on Baltimore Album quilts. In his own book, *Old Quilts,* published in 1946, he credited Marie

Webster with sparking his own interest in the subject.[7]

Now a prominent author, Marie Webster was invited to lecture and exhibit her work by every imaginable group, from the Mississippi Centennial Exposition to the Indianapolis Women's Prison. A hospital benefit in Illinois was more lavish than most: the hostess and guests were all attired in colonial style, although most of the hundred quilts on display had been made in the nineteenth century, not the colonial period. With an assistant dressed as "Aunt Jane of Kentucky," Marie gave her talk in a room furnished with heirlooms, including a melodeon, spinning wheel and a bunch of peacock feathers. This memorable event concluded with a demonstration of sampler making, a quilting song and a minuet.

To enhance her lectures, Marie Webster began to acquire her own small collection of quilts. Two came from women who had written to her from Hawaii. Dora Isenberg, from Lihue on the island of Kauai, offered to exchange an old Hawaiian quilt called "The Rain Falling in Honolulu" (Fig. 70) for two copies of *Quilts* and five patterns. Mary W. Deering of Honolulu wrote that Hawaiian quilts were selling there for $30, although there was "no place where they are on regular sale." In New York, Marie acquired a beautiful, though unfinished, white stuffed work quilt made in Greenwich Village in 1800. And from Texas came an exuberant nineteenth-century wedding quilt in an original tulip pattern with quilted hearts among the flowers.[8]

In 1917, when the United States entered the First World War, Marie became a Red Cross volunteer, knitting sweaters for the troops and teaching classes on how to make surgical dressings. *The Ladies' Home Journal*, exhorting its readers "to cheer and to strengthen the boy who has gone," published some of her knitwear patterns, but without her usual by-line.

During the war, she continued to create new quilts, experimenting with unusual sets and fabrics in Magpie Rose, Poinsettia (Plate 22) and Cherokee Rose. In 1917, Marion Wire wrote her from *The Journal*, "Mr. Bok asks me to get only the very newest things and naturally I must look all around. Will you please let me know if you have anything new in patchwork or other household needlework, or if among your friends there

MARIE D. WEBSTER
Marie Webster in the green silk colonial-style dress she wore when presenting her quilt lectures in the 1920s and 30s.

FIGURE 76

THREE EDITIONS OF *QUILTS*

A first edition of *Quilts: Their Story and How to Make Them,* in the center, is flanked by the 1926 Doubleday, Page & Company edition (left) and the 1929 edition which Marie Webster published herself.

FIGURE 77

POPPY PATTERN

Cardboard templates for the Poppy quilt pattern, used by Marie Webster and her partners in the Practical Patchwork Company when cutting fabrics for the kits they sold.

FIGURE 78

are any innovations in table linens?" Although Marie sent several quilts, they published just one, a new version of French Baskets, with roses instead of daisies, in February 1918.

In the 1920s, Marie Webster's pattern business entered a new period of expansion, evolving into a true cottage industry. It had started out strictly as a family business, with her son preparing the blueprints and her sister, Emma Daugherty, making the elaborate tissue paper patterns. But in 1921, she joined forces with two friends, Ida Hess and Evangeline Beshore, to found the Practical Patchwork Company. The new partners decided to specialize in basted quilts and kits of stamped or pre-cut fabric for bridge and luncheon sets as well as for bedspreads and quilts. Adopting the poetic motto, "A Thing of Beauty is a Joy Forever," they promoted their products through a series of catalogs and advertised in periodicals like *House Beautiful*. In addition to mail order, they sold through retail outlets like Eleanor Beard's Studio and the famous Mary A. McElwain Quilt & Gift Shop in Walworth, Wisconsin.[9]

In 1922, the *Marion Daily Chronicle* reported on their venture:

Of recent years the smartest and cleverest women have taken up various kinds of business, have entered most of the business fields and are showing their hitherto latent possibilities in the world from which they were so long barred by custom.

The paper quoted Ida Hess:

Art is best served when charm, beauty and utility are combined by the needle of the housewife in the articles she creates for the comfort and adornment of her home. Patchwork — one of the oldest forms of decoration — can now be so practically applied as to find instant favor with every woman who desires to create beautiful household furnishings of her own without undue effort. Not only is it gay and attractive, but patchwork is also a most practical art.

Unusual and varied articles suitable for the breakfast nook, the bridge table, and the tea service in the
sun-parlor can now be obtained with appropriate
decorations formed in this ancient method.[10]

With Marie Webster as designer, they offered an ever-
expanding line to their customers, with roses, wreaths and
flower baskets the most popular themes. In the 1920s, they
added eleven new patterns: Nasturtium Wreath, Clematis in
Bloom, Cluster of Roses, Dutch Baskets, May Tulips, Iris in
Baskets, Primrose Wreath, Pink Dogwood in Baskets, Wayside
Roses, Rainbow and Gay Garden (Plates 23–26, 28, 29). Prices
ranged from $100 for their most expensive finished quilt to a
modest $5 for a stamped kit with all materials for a baby quilt.
Recommended fabrics were the new colorfast cottons in a varied palette of solid pastels. The ambitious quiltmaker could
choose the pattern packet, complete with photo, pattern sheet,
directions, fabric swatches and colored tissue paper mock-up,
which still cost only 50 cents.

In the 1920s, as interest in quilting reached new heights,
media coverage dramatically increased. Even the *New York
Times* proclaimed "The Patchwork Quilt has a Revival" in its
review of a 1926 Arts Centre exhibit of historic pieces. In
Indiana, Marie Webster was featured in the local press as well
as in an *Indianapolis Star* article, "MARION, Known by her
Products." The picture of her quilts was captioned, "Patchwork
quilt, designed by Marie D. Webster, noted throughout the
world for her work." (Marion's other enterprises — the Delta
Electric Company, the National Sanatorium and the Indiana
Truck Corporation— proved much less photogenic!)[11]

Marie Webster was in even greater demand as a quilt judge
and speaker. When lecturing, she made a striking figure in her
colonial-style dress, "a quaint costume of years ago, made of
green silk, with wide lace collar, flowing bell sleeves, trimmed
in lace. In keeping with the times, her hair was dressed with
flowing curls about her shoulders" (Fig. 76). She was often
accompanied by a retinue of friends, who demonstrated quiltmaking and served tea, colorfully attired in fashions "of a
bygone day" — hoop skirts with lace mitts and parasols, or

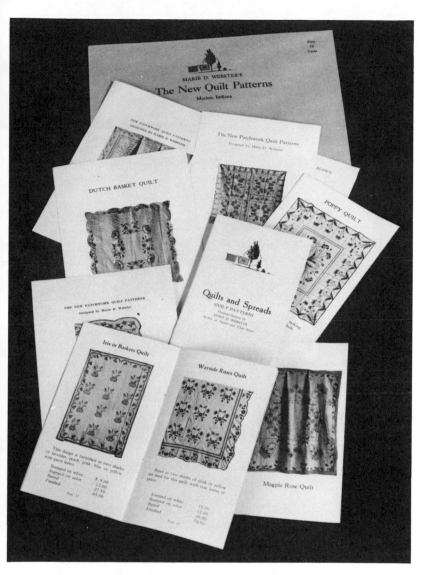

CATALOG AND LEAFLETS

Marie Webster's catalog entitled "Quilts and Spreads," a pattern envelope and leaflets showing several of her popular appliqué quilt designs.

FIGURE 79

PRACTICAL PATCHWORK AT THE FAIR

The Practical Patchwork Company set up this booth to display their quilts and other products at an Indiana county fair in the early 1920s.

FIGURE 80

calico and sunbonnets. Her partner, Evangeline Beshore, appeared in "tan silk with puffed sleeves, and a bonnet trimmed in baby blue ribbon to match," looking like "a picture from an old fashioned magazine."[12] Demand for quilt patterns soared and Marie Webster's designs began to appear again in the national magazines. The "Window Shopping" section of the October 1925 *House Beautiful* pictured May Tulips, Wreath of Roses and Morning Glory, suggesting, "These designs put up in attractive flowered boxes would make charming gifts for a bride's shower." *The Ladies' Home Journal* published another of her quilts, Pink Dogwood, in September 1927 and *Needlecraft* magazine offered patterns for Cherokee Rose in September 1930 and May Tulips in May 1931.

This renewed attention stimulated interest in *Quilts: Their Story and How to Make Them,* still the only full length book on the subject. Doubleday brought out a new edition in 1926, the first in a decade, which proved so popular that they reissued it in 1928. When that edition sold out within the year, Marie Webster arranged to publish the book herself in 1929, with a full page ad for her patterns on the back of the dust jacket.

Other pattern suppliers began to market the best-selling Webster designs, often failing to acknowledge their source. Quilt historian Cuesta Benberry has documented many instances, such as a 1928 Stearns and Foster "Mountain Mist" batting cover printed with Wind-blown Tulip, Iris and Sunflower. Although they later simplified the Sunflower design and substituted a different Iris pattern, Stearns and Foster has continued to sell the same Wind-blown Tulip pattern down to the present day. Sometimes the pattern names were changed: Mrs. Danner's Quilts of Emporia, Kansas, sold Webster's French Baskets as "Ivory Baskets" and the Lockport Cotton Company offered her Rainbow pattern under the name of "Spring Bouquet."[13]

By 1930, Marie Webster had been at the forefront of the quilt revival for twenty years. Now at the age of 70, she might have been expected to retire. Although she created no more new designs, she continued to run Practical Patchwork for another dozen years. Two younger women, Ida Lillard and

Gloria Eward, joined Evangeline Beshore and Emma Daugherty as partners in the company.

The heart of the business was the sunny spare room on the second floor of the Webster's house at 926 South Washington Street in Marion. There the women would gather to plan the day's work and visiting buyers would examine the colorful samples spread out on the bed. However, the home had one serious drawback as a workplace: it was right next to the railway line! The light-colored fabrics had to be protected at all costs from the soot filtering down over the neighborhood. Every evening, the work in progress was carefully put away in cardboard boxes which lined the closet shelves. When the quilt tops were finished, they were sent off to be quilted by professionals or church groups around the Midwest — in Kentucky, Indiana, Michigan and Kansas.

The 1930s brought several changes to the Webster family. In 1933, Lawrence married and moved back to Marion with his bride, Jeanette. In a few years, Marie Webster became the proud grandmother of two little girls. At last she indulged her love of travel, venturing to exotic destinations like Guatemala and South America, and fulfilled her life's ambition to visit Egypt and the Mediterranean. On a sadder note, George became seriously ill and died in 1938. Marie and her sister, Emma, remained in the big house, with Lawrence living right around the corner.

In 1942, when Lawrence and his family moved to the quiet college town of Princeton, New Jersey, Marie and her sister packed up their quilts and joined them. After being in business for thirty years, they were glad to retire, though sorry to leave their close friends behind. Evangeline Beshore continued to run Practical Patchwork from her home for a few more years until she, too, retired.

During World War II, Marie invited a group of women to meet weekly at the Webster home to make clothes for the refugee children of a war-torn Europe. Although she no longer made quilts, she still corresponded with quilt lovers from around the world and was pleased to learn that her book was still in demand. The Tudor Publishing Company of New York reprinted it twice, in 1943 and 1948.

Marie Webster retained her grace, wit and keen intellect even into her 90s. Exceptionally active for a person of her age, she still loved to sew — whether new curtains for the house or tiny dresses for her granddaughters' dolls. She was still an avid reader, concert-goer and traveler, making trips to New York City and even to Indiana. Then, in the mid-1950s, she suffered a severe stroke from which she did not recover. She died on August 29, 1956, shortly after her 97th birthday.

Her impact on the quilt world was far-reaching. Through her magazine articles, her book and, on a more personal level, through her talks, she awakened a wide audience to the artistry of quilts and the richness of our quiltmaking heritage. Her book was the first to study women and their quilts, greatly influencing later writers on the subject. Its illustrations have delighted countless readers over the years.

She revitalized the tradition of appliqué and spearheaded a new style of natural forms in soft harmonious colors. Her simple yet effective designs have been interpreted by some of the nation's finest quiltmakers and are still popular today, appearing in the leading quilt magazines.[14] But perhaps her greatest achievement of all was simply to inspire women to make quilts, creating a legacy of beauty for people everywhere.

NOTES

1. Quilt features in *The Ladies' Home Journal* included Sybil Lanigan's "Revival of the Patchwork Quilt," October 1894; Jane Benson, "Designs for Patchwork Quilt," November 1896. Then, in 1905, a series of original quilt designs by well known artists: Ernest Thompson Seton, "A Wild-Animal Bedquilt"; Maxfield Parrish, "A Circus Bedquilt"; Gazo Foudji, "A Dragon Bedquilt"; Peter Newell, "An Alice in Wonderland Bedquilt"; Jessie Willcox Smith, "A Child's Good-Night Bedquilt." (These five designs were so complicated that the magazine was unable to offer patterns to its readers.) Also, Lilian Barton Wilson, "Some New Designs in Patchwork," Oct. 1907; Mrs. Leopold Simon, "When Patchwork Becomes An Art," Aug. 1908; Elizabeth Daingerfield, "Kentucky Mountain Patchwork Quilts," July 1909, and "The Kentucky Mountain Quilt," Feb. 1912. (For more on Elizabeth Daingerfield, see Chapter IV, note 10.)

2. See Figure 64 for a photograph of Mrs. Helm, superintendent of the residence for elderly women, at her quilting frame.

3. *Marion Daily Chronicle*, 10 Feb. 1911.

4. Outline embroidery patterns for bonneted girls based on Kate Greenaway's drawings were widely sold in the late 1800s and were often used to embellish Crazy Quilts. The Ladies' Art Company catalog published a number of sunbonnet figures derived from Bertha Corbett's and Bernhardt Wall's illustrations. See Dolores A. Hinson, *The Sunbonnet Family of Quilt Patterns* (New York: Prentice Hall, 1983), Cuesta Benberry, "The Paradox of the Sunbonnet Girl Quilt Pattern," *Quilters' Journal*, Vol. 2, no. 1, and Betty J. Hagerman, *A Meeting of the Sunbonnet Children* (Baldwin City, KS: Betty J. Hagerman, 1979).

5. This clipping and the letters and reviews quoted below were among the items Marie Webster kept in her scrapbook, later donated by her daughter-in-law, Jeanette Scott Thurber, to the Indianapolis Museum of Art. (See note 14 below.)

6. George H. Ketcham (1862–1925) was equally renowned as a sportsman (both yachting and horse racing) and as proprietor of the Valentine Company, the foremost chain of theaters in the Midwest. "He was an earnest collector of objects of art and had a penchant for old fashioned quilts which he considered a product of early American art."

His collection, containing "the finest and most historical examples extant," was exhibited at the Toledo Museum of Art in 1923–24 (*Toledo Times*, 30 July 1925). According to Cuesta Benberry, after his death this historic collection was dispersed at auction.

7. Dr. William Rush Dunton, Jr. (1868–1966) was a pioneer in the development of occupational therapy. He was a prolific writer, who often recommended quilting as a therapeutic activity. See *Occupation Therapy: A Manual for Nurses* (Philadelphia: W.B. Saunders Company, 1915) and two articles in *Occupational Therapy and Rehabilitation:* "Quilts and Quilting," June 1930 (co-authored by his wife, Edna H. Dunton), and "Quilt Making as a Socializing Measure," August 1937.

8. Both the white quilt and the Texas wedding quilt are in the Webster Collection at the Indianapolis Museum of Art.

9. John Keats' lines from Book I of *Endymion* seem especially appropriate to the subject of quilts:

> A thing of beauty is a joy for ever:
> Its loveliness increases; it will never
> Pass into nothingness; but still will keep
> A bower quiet for us, and a sleep
> Full of sweet dreams, and health,
>   and quiet breathing.

Marie Webster began publishing four-page descriptions of "The New Patchwork Quilt Patterns" about 1918. The Practical Patchwork Company expanded these into 16 to 20-page illustrated catalogs entitled "Quilts and Spreads."

See also two articles by Cuesta Benberry: "Quilt Cottage Industries: A Chronicle" in *Uncoverings, 1986* (Mill Valley, CA: American Quilt Study Group, 1987) and "Marie D. Webster," *Quilter's Newsletter Magazine*, planned for July/Aug. 1990. For more about Mary McElwain see "Memories of Mary A. McElwain Quilt Shop" by Ruth W. Peterson in *Quilters' Journal*, #24. Her shop was founded in 1912 and was still in business in 1952, offering the quilting of tops as well as a wide selection of finished quilts. Mary McElwain published her own catalog of Webster quilt kits and in 1936, a book, *The Romance of the Village Quilts*.

10. *Marion Daily Chronicle*, 8 Nov. 1922.

11. *New York Times*, 25 July 1926; *Marion Daily Chronicle*, 28 May 1925; *Indianapolis Star*, 12 July 1925.

12. *Marion Leader-Tribune*, 12 Nov. 1924; 24 Sept. 1925.

13. Cuesta Benberry, "Stearns and Foster," Part 3, *Quilters' Journal,* Vol. 4, no. 2, 1981, and "Marie D. Webster," *Quilter's Newsletter Magazine,* planned for July/August 1990.

14. Ten of Marie Webster's quilts are in the collection of the Indianapolis Museum of Art, a gift from her daughter-in-law, Jeanette Scott Thurber: American Beauty Rose, originally called "Pink Rose" (Plate 1), Sunflower (Plate 8), Daisies (Plate 12), Morning Glory Wreath (Plate 13), Bedtime (Plate 14), Grapes and Vines (Plate 16), Magpie Rose, Poinsettia (Plate 22), Primrose Wreath (Plate 24) and May Tulips.

Webster patterns have been used by master quiltmakers like Rose Kretsinger (Wreath of Roses, Spencer Museum of Art, University of Kansas), Charlotte Jane Whitehill (Wreath of Roses, Denver Art Museum), Mary Schafer (Grapes and Vines) and Dr. Jeannette Dean-Throckmorton (Iris, Art Institute of Chicago).

Some Webster designs published in recent issues of quilt magazines include: *Quilter's Newsletter,* Wind-blown Tulip (May 1978), Wreath of Roses (Sept. 1978), Morning Glory Wreath (Sept. 1979); *Quilt,* May Tulips, called "Tulip Garland" (Summer 1985); *Lady's Circle Patchwork Quilts,* Wreath of Roses (Spring 1983), Poppy (Fall 1984), May Tulips, (May 1985), Primrose Wreath, called "Blue Prim Rose" (Nov. 1986), Pink Dogwood, called "Basket and Dogwood" (Dec. 1986). Quilts based on her Poppy and Pink Dogwood patterns have even appeared in a Japanese magazine, *Patchwork Quilt Tsushin*, No. 29, 1989.

BIBLIOGRAPHY

Addison, Julia de Wolf. *Arts and Crafts in the Middle Ages.* London: G. Bell, 1908.

Archer, Thomas A. and Charles L. Kingsford. *The Crusades: The Story of the Latin Kingdom of Jerusalem.* New York: Putnam's, 1894.

Benberry, Cuesta. "An Historic Quilt Document: The Ladies Art Company Catalog." *Quilters' Journal,* Vol. 1, no. 4, Summer 1978, pp. 13–14.

——— . "Marie D. Webster." *Quilter's Newsletter Magazine,* planned for July/Aug. 1990.

——— . "Marie D. Webster Quilt Patterns." *Nimble Needle Treasures,* Vol. 7, no. 2, 1975, pp. 1–4.

——— . "Missouri: 20th Century Quilt Pattern Supplier." *Lady's Circle Patchwork Quilts,* May 1988, pp. 38–39, 42–43, 57.

——— . "Quilt Cottage Industries: A Chronicle." In *Uncoverings 1986.* Mill Valley, CA: American Quilt Study Group, 1987.

——— . "Stearns and Foster." Part 3. *Quilters' Journal,* Vol. 4, no. 2, 1981, pp. 13–15.

——— . "The 20th Century's First Quilt Revival." Parts 1–3. *Quilter's Newsletter,* July/Aug. 1979, pp. 20–22; Sept. 1979, pp. 25–26; Oct. 1979, pp. 10–11, 37.

Benberry, Cuesta and Joyce Gross. "Cuesta Benberry, Part II: Significant Milestones for Quilters." *Quilters' Journal,* March 1984, p. 7.

Brackman, Barbara. *Clues in the Calico: A Guide to Identifying and Dating Antique Quilts.* McLean, VA: EPM Publications, 1989.

Burton, Margaret S. "Old Bed-spreads, Quilts, and Coverlets — An Alluring Field for the Collector." *Country Life in America,* 15 Dec. 1910, pp. 197–198.

Christie, Grace. *Embroidery and Tapestry Weaving.* London: J. Hogg, 1915.

Cole, Alan S. "Old Embroideries." Parts 1–3. *Home Needlework Magazine,* July 1900, pp. 173–183; Oct. 1900, pp. 263–272; Jan. 1901, pp. 3–14.

Daingerfield, Elizabeth. "Patch Quilts and Philosophy." *Craftsman,* Aug. 1908, pp. 523–527.

———. "Kentucky Mountain Patchwork Quilts." *The Ladies' Home Journal,* July 1909.

———. "The Kentucky Mountain Quilt." *The Ladies' Home Journal,* Feb. 1912, p. 46.

Davison, Mildred. *American Quilts.* Chicago: Art Institute of Chicago, 1966.

Day, Lewis F. and Mary Buckle. *Art in Needlework.* London: B.T. Batsford, 1900.

Dyer, Walter A. *The Lure of the Antique.* New York: The Century Co., 1910.

Earle, Alice Morse. *Customs and Fashions in Old New England.* New York: Scribner's, 1893.

———. *Colonial Days in Old New York.* 1896. Reprint edition, Port Washington, NY: Ira J. Friedman, 1962.

———. *Home Life in Colonial Days.* New York: Macmillan, 1898.

Garnett, Lucy M. *Turkey of the Ottomans.* New York: Scribner's, 1911.

Gibbons, Phebe Earle. *"Pennsylvania Dutch" and Other Essays.* Philadelphia: Lippincott, 1882.

Glaister, Elizabeth. *Needlework.* London: Macmillan, 1880.

Hall, Eliza Calvert. *Aunt Jane of Kentucky.* Boston: Little, Brown, 1907.

Harrison, Constance Cary. *Woman's Handiwork in Modern Homes.* New York: Scribner's, 1881.

Holme, Charles, ed. *Peasant Art in Sweden, Lapland and Iceland.* London: The Studio, 1910.

Holme, Geoffrey, ed. *A Book of Old Embroidery*. London: The Studio, 1921.

Hughes, Therle. *English Domestic Needlework, 1660–1860*. New York, Macmillan, 1961.

Jones, Mary Eirwen. *A History of Western Embroidery*. London: Studio Vista, 1969.

Josephus. *The Jewish War*. Translated by G. A. Williamson. Harmondsworth: Penguin Books, 1970.

Jourdain, Margaret. *English Secular Embroidery*. New York: E.P. Dutton, 1912.

Joyce, Patrick Weston. *A Social History of Ancient Ireland*. 1913. 2 vols. Reprint edition, New York: Benjamin Blom, 1968.

Levering, Julia H. *Historic Indiana*. New York: Putnam's, 1916.

Lowes, Emily Leigh *Chats on Old Lace and Needlework*. New York: Frederick A. Stokes, 1908.

Locke, John. "Some Thoughts Concerning Education." In *The Educational Writings of John Locke,* edited by James L. Axtell. Cambridge: Cambridge University Press, 1968.

Marston, Gwen and Joe Cunningham. *American Beauties: Rose and Tulip Quilts*. Paducah, KY: American Quilter's Society, 1988.

———. *Sets and Borders*. Paducah, KY: American Quilter's Society, 1987.

Martin, Nancy J. *Pieces of the Past*. Bothell, WA: That Patchwork Place, 1986.

McKown, June R. *Marion: A Pictorial History*. St. Louis: G. Bradley Publishing, 1989.

Morley, Margaret W. *The Carolina Mountains*. Boston: Houghton Mifflin, 1913.

Perrot, Georges and Charles Chipiez. *Histoire de l'Art Dans L'Antiquité*. 10 vols. Paris: Librairie Hachette, 1882–1914.

Ramsey, James G. M. *The Annals of Tennessee to the End of the Eighteenth Century*. 1853. Reprint edition, New York: Arno Press, 1971.

Ridlon, Gideon Tibbetts. *Saco Valley Settlements and Families.* 1895. Reprint edition, Rutland, VT: Charles E. Tuttle, 1969.

Robertson, Elizabeth Wells. *American Quilts.* New York: Studio Publications, 1948.

Rock, Daniel. *Textile Fabrics.* South Kensington Museum Art Handbooks No. 1. New York: Scribner, Welford & Armstrong, 1876.

Schuette, Marie and Sigrid Müller-Christensen. *A Pictorial History of Embroidery.* New York: Frederick A. Praeger, 1964.

Shackleton, Robert and Elizabeth F. *The Quest of the Colonial.* New York: Century Co., 1907.

Smith, Helen Evertson. *Colonial Days and Ways.* New York: Century Co., 1900.

Stickley, Gustav. *Craftsman Homes: Architecture and Furnishings of the American Arts and Crafts Movement.* 1909. Reprint edition, New York: Dover Publications, 1979.

Stowe, Harriet Beecher. *The Minister's Wooing.* New York: Derby & Jackson, 1859.

[Strauss, Juliet V.] *The Ideas of a Plain Country Woman.* By "The Country Contributor." New York: Doubleday, Page & Co., 1908.

Swain, Margaret H. *Historical Needlework.* London: Barrie & Jenkins, 1970.

————. *The Needlework of Mary Queen of Scots.* New York: Van Nostrand Reinhold, 1973.

Taylor, John. "The Praise of the Needle." In *Works of John Taylor, the Water Poet.* Spenser Society, 1870. Reprint edition, New York: Burt Franklin, 1967.

Todd, Charles Burr. *The Story of the City of New York.* New York: Putnam's, 1888.

Vallois, Grace M. *First Steps in Collecting.* London: T. Werner Laurie, 1913.

Vanderbilt, Gertrude Lefferts. *The Social History of Flatbush.* New York: D. Appleton, 1881.

Wardle, Patricia. *Guide to English Embroidery*. London: Her Majesty's Stationery Office, 1970.

Webster, Marie D. "The New Patchwork Quilt." *The Ladies' Home Journal*, 1 Jan. 1911, p. 25.

―――. "The New Patchwork Cushions." *The Ladies' Home Journal*, Aug. 1911, p. 25.

―――. "The New Flower Patchwork Quilts." *The Ladies' Home Journal*, Jan. 1912, p. 38.

―――. "The Baby's Patchwork Quilt." *The Ladies' Home Journal*, Aug. 1912, p. 27.

―――. "A Rose Patchwork Bedroom." *The Ladies' Home Journal*, Oct. 1915, p. 43.

―――. *Quilts: Their Story and How to Make Them*. Garden City, NY: Doubleday, Page & Co., 1915; London: B. T. Batsford.

―――. *Quilts: Their Story and How to Make Them*. Garden City, NY: Doubleday, Page & Co., 1926.

―――. *Quilts: Their Story and How to Make Them*. Marion, IN: Marie D.Webster, 1929.

―――. *Quilts: Their Story and How to Make Them*. New York: Tudor Publishing, 1943.

―――. *Quilts: Their Story and How to Make Them*. Detroit: Gale Research, 1972.

―――. "The Coverlet and Cushion." *The Ladies' Home Journal*, Feb. 1918, p. 110.

―――. "Window Shopping." *House Beautiful*, Oct. 1925, p. 322.

―――. "Pink Dogwood in Appliqué for the Bedroom." *The Ladies' Home Journal*, Sept. 1927, p. 92.

―――. "The Cherokee Rose Quilt." *Needlecraft Magazine*, Sept. 1930, p. 25. Reprinted in *Quilter's Newsletter Magazine*, May 1985, p. 42.

―――. "The May Tulip Quilt in Applique." *Needlecraft Magazine*, May 1931, p. 6.

Whitson, Rolland Lewis. *Centennial History of Grant County.* 2 vols. Chicago: Lewis Publishing, 1914.

Wilkinson, Sir John Gardner. *A Popular Account of the Ancient Egyptians.* 2 vols. New York: Harper & Bros., 1854.

Wilson, Lilian Barton. "Appliqué Embroidery on Linen." *The Ladies' Home Journal,* Jan. 1908, p. 41.

Wilton, Countess of, ed. *The Art of Needlework.* London: H. Colburn, 1840.

Woodard, Thomas K. and Blanche Greenstein. *Twentieth Century Quilts, 1900–1950.* New York: E.P. Dutton, 1988.

INDEX

INDEX OF QUILT NAMES

*See also Chapter VI, pp. 115–132, and List of Quilt Names,
Arranged Alphabetically, pp. 169–176*

Photo: Wm. B. Dewey

ROSALIND WEBSTER PERRY was born in Marion, Indiana, and grew up in Princeton, New Jersey, with her parents, sister and famous grandmother, Marie Webster. A graduate of Wellesley College, she has an M.A. in philosophy from the University of London. She is married to writer and artist Richard Perry; they have two daughters and live in Santa Barbara, California.

Richard and Rosalind are collaborating on a series of illustrated guides to the colonial architecture of Mexico. The first, *Maya Missions*, about the churches of Yucatan, was published in 1988. Rosalind is also co-author of *California's Chumash Indians,* in conjunction with the Santa Barbara Museum of Natural History.

Photo Credits
Bill Boyd: Plates 20, 21, 27
Wm. B. Dewey: Plates 15, 19, 35; Figs. 77–79
Myron Miller: Plates 17, 23, 25, 26, 28, 29, 32
Moore Photography: Plate 33
Pamela Mougin: Plates 30, 31
Bill Myers: Plate 36

Color Separations by Santa Barbara Photo Engraving

Typography by Tom Buhl Typographers

Publications from **Practical Patchwork:**

QUILTS: Their Story and How to Make Them

A new edition of America's first quilt book
by Marie Webster. With a biography of the author
and numerous color plates of her own quilts.

Cloth: $30.00   Paper: $18.00   Plus $2.50 shipping
(California Residents, please add local sales tax.)

Marie Webster's Quilt Patterns

This attractive 5-page brochure illustrates, for
the first time, all Marie Webster's classic designs.
A valuable resource for the quilt enthusiast.

(Black & White) $2.50 postpaid

Forthcoming:

A Joy Forever

The first Marie Webster pattern book.
Scheduled for 1991, this book is based on the original
appliqué designs of this influential pioneer of the early
20th century quilt revival.

Available from   **Practical Patchwork**
P. O. Box 30065
Santa Barbara, CA 93130